FASTLANE FORTUNE

DRIVE

YOUR WAY TO FINANCIAL FREEDOM

BY KATHY R. ORRELL

FASTLANE FORTUNE

Copyright © [2024] by [EDWARD N. ORR]

All rights reserved. No part of this publication may be reproduced, distributed, or transmitted in any form or by any means, including photocopying, recording, or other electronic or mechanical methods, without the prior written permission of the publisher, except in the case of brief quotations embodied in critical reviews and certain other noncommercial uses permitted by copyright law.

DISCLIAMER

The techniques in this book are meant to maximise your financial potential. Personal financial decisions are complicated and particular to each person, though. The counsel in this book is meant to be informative and instructive; it is not to be regarded as professional, legal, or financial advice. Before making any financial decisions, please speak with a licenced expert.

ACKNOWLEDGEMENT

Writing this book has been a life-changing experience made feasible by the encouragement, direction, and help of many people.

Above all, I would want to sincerely thank the pioneers in the fields of business and financial independence, whose groundbreaking writings have greatly impacted my life and inspired me to start my writing career. To Robert Kiyosaki, whose groundbreaking book Rich Dad Poor Dad let me realise what financial literacy and freedom might do. To Tim Ferriss, who showed me the value of productivity tricks and lifestyle design in The 4-Hour Workweek. Dedicated to MJ DeMarco, whose The Millionaire Fastlane offered the fundamental ideas that guide much of the thinking in this book. I now understand wealth development and financial independence much better because of your knowledge and thoughts.

I also like to thank Napoleon Hill whose ageless book Think and Grow Rich has served as a source of inspiration and mental toughness. Your lectures on the importance of perseverance and attitude have been a lighthouse for me during this journey.

Thanks especially to T. Harv Eker, whose Secrets of the Millionaire Mind have significantly changed the way I think about wealth principles and financial psychology. My path has benefited much from your ideas on money management techniques and financial plans.

It would be wrong of me to overlook Peter Thiel, whose Zero to One has encouraged me to think creatively and approach entrepreneurship from a new angle. The strategic aspects of this book have been much impacted by your views on constructing the future and generating distinctive value.

I am so very grateful to my wonderful family for your constant support and encouragement that words cannot adequately convey. I owe my parents for fostering in me the principles of perseverance, hard effort, and the conviction that I could accomplish anything I put my mind too. My foundation has been your unending love and sacrifices.

Thank you to my husband for your endless hours of writing and rewriting, for your understanding and patience. My greatest source of power has been your unwavering support and belief in my goal. Thank you to my kids for your never-ending curiosity and for helping me to remember how important it is to have great dreams and live passionately. Most inspiring are your happiness and excitement.

And last, thank you to my friends and coworkers who have supported, inspired, and given me priceless criticism along the road. This effort has been refined and brought to completion in large part because of your support and insights.

The knowledge and encouragement of all the amazing people in my life are collectively reflected in this book. I appreciate your belief in me and your contribution to realising this ambition.

FASTLANE FORTUNE

Table of Contents

INTRODUCTION 7

CHAPTER ONE 13

The Need for Speed 13

Exploring the Limitations of Traditional Financial Advice 16

Why Speed is Crucial for Building Wealth 18

The Fast lane Advantage: Using Speed to Your Advantage 22

CHAPTER 2 28

Assessing Demand and Market Potential 36

Selecting Your Fast lane Route: Investing, Business, or Both 43

CHAPTER 3 50

Making Assets Work for You: Leveraging Systems** 62

Using Other People's Resources: Money, Time, and Knowledge 68

CHAPTER 4 77

The Wealth Acceleration Commandments 77

DRIVE YOUR WAY INTO FINANCIAL FREEDOM

Manage Time, Manage Wealth................... 86

Solve Needs, Reap Rewards 89

Growth Is Required: Scale or Fail................ 94

CHAPTER 5 98

FASTLANE STRATEGIES 98

CHAPTER 6 107

Fueling Your Fastlane Journey: Strategies for Sustainable Growth 107

Developing Routines for Optimal Output and Efficiency* 112

Sustainable Speed in the Balance: Long-Term Wealth vs Short-Term Gains 116

CHAPTER 7 120

Moving Through the Fast Lane: Effective Success Techniques 120

Methods for Balancing Speed and Sustainability. 124

Wealth Management: From Income Creation to Asset Defence 128

Opening Up Your Fastlane Experience** 131

FASTLANE FORTUNE

INTRODUCTION

Frustrated, a young businesswoman named Sarah sat with her laptop in a little, busy coffee shop in the middle of the city. Even with her diligence and commitment, she was still unable to achieve her goal of financial independence. She had studied several personal finance books and adhered to every conventional piece of advice, yet she was still stuck in the slow lane, crawling along a route that would only yield success after decades of hard work. That is, until she happened onto "The Fastlane: Drive Your Way to Financial Freedom," a book that would completely transform her life.

A Change in Paradigm

Imagine a world in which retirement is not a far-off dream but rather a reality soon enough, where you are not dependent on the arduous grind of a 9–5 job, and where your financial success is not tied to the meagre yearly rises that you receive. Not only is "The Fastlane" a book, but it's also an awakening that contradicts everything of the conventional wisdom regarding prosperity and self-sufficiency. The self-made billionaire author debunks the fallacies surrounding conventional wealth-building strategies and presents a road map that will enable you to become financially independent sooner than you ever would have imagined.

The Slow Lane and the Sidewalk Illusion

Either the Sidewalk or the Slow Lane is where most of us end up. People that live paycheck to paycheck, spend carelessly, and save nothing are the people who crowd the sidewalk. It's a route filled with reckless spending and quick satisfaction that will inevitably result in financial disaster. Sarah has witnessed a great deal of her friends being hooked on this path, never looking past the next high.

And then there's the Slow Lane, which Sarah had been taking quite seriously. This is the path that the general public advocates: secure employment, careful saving, mutual fund investments, and the belief that compound interest will do its magic over the course of forty years. It's a route of postponed satisfaction, with decades between promises of financial independence. However, taking the Slow Lane comes with its own set of risks. The merciless math of inflation, job uncertainty, and economic downturns can all ruin even the best-laid plans.

Finding the Quick Lane

Sarah was looking through her social media account one gloomy afternoon when she came across a message that caught her attention. It was a success story about a guy who, instead of taking the Slow Lane and reaching financial independence in his 30s, chose to take what he called the "Fastlane." She followed the link out of curiosity and found herself on a blog post that went over the main ideas of "The Fastlane: Drive Your Way to Financial Freedom."

The idea of the book was straightforward but revolutionary: one might quickly become financially independent, but doing so would need adopting a new perspective and being willing to defy social conventions. In The Fastlane, we will discuss how to use entrepreneurship to create explosive riches, how to take advantage of scale, and why value creation is so important.

A Fastlaner's Mindset

The book emphasises that adopting a Fastlaner's perspective is the first stage. Fastlaners think and behave with a sense of urgency and purpose, in contrast to Sidewalkers who live for the moment and Slowlaners who dream about the future. They want to double their time and efforts through astute commercial tactics rather than just exchanging time for money.

Sarah discovered that a fast-paced individual sees opportunities and ways to provide value in the world. Instead than thinking, "How can I earn a steady paycheck?" they ask, "How can I create something that solves a problem for many people?" The secret to unlocking the door to exponential financial growth was this change of mindset.

The Road Map for Fastlane

A detailed road plan for moving from the Slow Lane to the Fast Lane is provided in the book. It's not about betting your cash on get-rich-quick schemes or taking careless chances. Rather, the focus is on deliberate, purposeful acts that efficiently utilise resources, time, and effort.

1. **Identify a Need**: Quick learners are skilled at identifying issues that require attention. They are aware that value is the source of money flow. Sarah came to the realisation that she needed to identify a problem that she could solve in a special and expandable way.

2. **Create Value**: Following the identification of a need, the next stage is to develop a good or service that addresses that need more effectively than anything that is already on the market. This could be accomplished by unparalleled customer service, innovation, or excellent quality.

3. **Leverage Scale:** Scale is where the Fastlane really shines. Fastlaners strive to service numerous clients at a reasonable price as opposed to a small number of clients at an exorbitant fee. Sarah found that the internet was an effective instrument for

FASTLANE FORTUNE

inexpensively reaching a worldwide audience.

4. **Protect Your Wealth**: Making money fast is one thing; safeguarding it is quite another. The necessity of prudent money management, reinvesting in your company, and generating numerous sources of income is emphasised throughout the book.

The Fastlane Success Pillars

Sarah became absorbed in the book's tenets, which outlined the five fundamental foundations that any prosperous freelancer built upon:

1. Education : Self-directed study as opposed to traditional, degree-focused instruction. In order to stay competitive, fast-leavers are lifelong learners who are always picking up new abilities and information.

2. Mindset: It's important to have a resilient, growth-oriented mindset. Only those who can continue and adapt will succeed on the difficult path to financial freedom.

3. Productivity: Time and resource management must be done with efficiency. Experts in efficiency, freelancers constantly seek methods to maximise their output and complete tasks in a shorter amount of time.

4. Marketing : No matter how excellent your product or service is, it won't sell if no one knows about it. Expanding and getting in front of more people requires efficient marketing.

5. Sales: One of the most important skills is the ability to market yourself, your service, and even your product. Sales psychology is something that freelancers are aware of and take advantage of.

Actual Fast-Traveled Success Stories

FASTLANE FORTUNE

The real-life success tales in the book added to Sarah's interest in it. They were neither fictitious instances nor wealthy celebrities. These were just regular people who had achieved exceptional outcomes by applying the concepts of Fastlane. These success stories—from the young couple who launched a multimillion-dollar e-commerce company to the single mother who built an online course empire—served as tangible evidence that the Fastlane was a practical route to financial independence rather than only a notion.

Surmounting Fear and Acting

Sarah discovered as she read more in the book that fear was one of the main barriers to accessing the Fastlane. dread of not succeeding, dread of not knowing what lies ahead, and anxiety of moving from the security of a consistent salary. Rather than avoiding this fact, the book provided helpful guidance on conquering these anxieties.

It urged readers to push the limits of their comfort zones on a regular basis, accept failure as a teaching opportunity, and take measured risks. Sarah became aware of her own anxieties and the justifications she had come up with over the years. It was time to put the dreams aside and get to work.

A Brand-New Adventure

Encouraged and energised, Sarah made the decision to go on. She started by determining her interests and abilities, searching for areas where she might add value. She launched a tiny online business and used digital marketing and social media to connect with her target market. She experienced many sleepless nights and arduous labour, but she felt in control of her financial future for the first time.

FASTLANE FORTUNE

She followed the book's guidelines at every turn, from arranging productive workflows to sensibly reinvesting earnings. Her business, along with her self-assurance and stable finances, expanded gradually but steadily. She was accumulating wealth rather than just making money.

You're in the fast lane

"The Fastlane: Drive Your Way to Financial Freedom" is an immersive experience as well as a book. Anyone who is ready to embrace a quicker, more active way to financial security and is sick of the sluggish, uncertain path should take note of this call to action. The Fastlane provides a road map for realising your aspirations, whether you're an employee looking for a promotion, an ambitious business owner, or just someone looking for a better life.

The trip to financial freedom is not simple, as Sarah's tale demonstrates, but it is possible to overcome the limitations of the conventional financial paths and move faster towards actual riches and independence with the correct attitude, information, and willpower. Your Fastlane voyage is waiting for you, the road is wide open, and the opportunities are limitless. Are you prepared to drive?

CHAPTER ONE

The Need for Speed

In a Slow-Lane World

Imagine this: You're crawling along at a snail's pace in the slow lane of life, caught in bumper to bumper traffic. You've been saving for retirement, getting a job, going to school, and crossing your fingers. These are the standard financial guidelines. You know in your heart, though, that there must be a better way.

Surviving the Financial Deadlock

Welcome to the Fastlane, where quickness is of the essence and there are new regulations. We'll look at why following the conventional wisdom to "save, invest, and wait" could be getting you stuck in a financial rut in this chapter. We'll reveal the drawbacks of the leisurely pace and explain why it's necessary to change course and pursue a quicker, more thrilling route to financial success.

FASTLANE FORTUNE

The Significance of Speed

It's all about the moment in the Fast lane. We'll explore the reasons why attaining financial wealth and freedom requires speed. You'll learn how to get from where you are to where you want to be much faster by ramping up your wealth-building efforts.

The Benefit of the Fast Lane

However, what makes the Fast lane preferable to the sidewalk or the slow lane? We'll talk about the special benefits of this nontraditional strategy for building wealth. You'll discover why the Fast lane provides a path to financial independence that conventional approaches just cannot match, from employing cutting-edge tactics to maximising the force of velocity.

Adopting the Need for Quickness

Now is the moment to start your engines and give in to your urge for speed. This chapter will motivate you to question the current quo, take a risk, and set out on an exciting journey to financial freedom. Fast lane is

FASTLANE FORTUNE

waiting for you, so fasten your seatbelt and get ready to move from the slow lane.

FASTLANE FORTUNE

Exploring the Limitations of Traditional Financial Advice

Assume that achieving financial success is as easy as according to a set of tried-and-true guidelines: enroll in education, get employment, save regularly, make prudent investments, and enjoy a comfortable retirement. It's a reassuring story that offers stability and security in an unpredictable world. But a closer look reveals the shortcomings and restrictions of this conventional wealth-building strategy.

Traditional financial advice is fundamentally based on the idea of playing things safe and adhering to a tried-and-true route to financial security. But what if genuine prosperity is sacrificed in the sake of safety? What if the guidelines we've been taught to adhere to really make it harder for us to reach our financial goals?

The emphasis of conventional financial advice on gradual growth is one of its most obvious drawbacks. Although placing a strong emphasis on long-term savings and cautious investments may provide security, doing so also necessitates tolerating a sluggish pace of wealth increase. Many people perceive this slow-lane strategy as more of a crawl than a sprint in their quest for financial independence.

Furthermore, the ability of entrepreneurship and innovation to create wealth is frequently overlooked in traditional financial advice. Although investing and saving have a place, they are not as beneficial as the possibility of quickly accelerating wealth that comes with launching a business or making high-growth investments. If we follow the conventional playbook to the letter, we might miss out on the Fastlane's tremendous potential.

The one-size-fits-all nature of conventional financial advice is another drawback. A seasoned business owner aiming to grow their company may not find value in the guidance offered to a young professional just beginning their career. However, conventional wisdom ignores these variations in situation and gives general guidance that doesn't connect with people on their particular financial paths.

Why Speed is Crucial for Building Wealth

In the world of wealth creation, time is not just valuable – it's the most precious asset you have. Every moment spent idly waiting for your investments to grow is a missed opportunity to accelerate your journey toward financial freedom. That's where the idea of speed becomes crucial – the capacity to quickly grow your wealth and reach your financial objectives in a fraction of the time it would take through conventional methods.

Capitalizing on Compound Growth

Speed is crucial because it is rooted in the concept of exponential growth. Compound interest is widely recognized as a remarkable phenomenon, and it's easy to see why. By reinvesting your earnings and allowing them to compound over time, you can exponentially increase your wealth. However, the true power of compounding lies in its ability to accelerate – the faster your investments grow, the more they can compound, leading to exponential gains that far outstrip the slow and steady approach advocated by traditional financial advice.

FASTLANE FORTUNE

Seizing Opportunities

In the dynamic realm of wealth creation, opportunities swiftly arise and vanish. In the world of finance, timing is everything. Whether it's a promising stock, a profitable business venture, or an exceptional investment opportunity, acting swiftly can make or break your chances of success. Those who move quickly can capitalize on these opportunities and turn them into massive gains, while those who hesitate are left watching from the sidelines.

Adapting to Market Changes

The financial markets are constantly evolving, and those who can't keep up are destined to be left behind. Speed is essential for staying ahead of the curve and adapting to changes in market conditions. Whether it's shifting investment strategies, pivoting your business model, or seizing new opportunities as they arise, the ability to move quickly is crucial for navigating the ever-changing landscape of wealth creation.

Breaking Through Plateaus

In the journey toward financial freedom, it's not uncommon to hit plateaus – periods where your progress stalls, and it feels like you're stuck in neutral. Speed is the key to breaking through these plateaus and propelling yourself to new heights of wealth and success. By taking decisive action and embracing the need for speed, you can overcome obstacles, push past limitations, and achieve levels of wealth you never thought possible

Unleashing Momentum's Power

Consider the production of wealth as a snowball sliding down a hill. It begins modest at first, but with each revolution, it gets exponentially bigger as it gathers velocity. In a similar vein, you can create greater momentum the faster you speed your wealth-building endeavours. This momentum turns into a strong force that pushes you in the direction of your financial objectives and increases your speed and efficiency.

Using the Advantage of Being First to Market

Being first usually translates into being the greatest in the quick-paced realm of creating riches. Early adopters who take advantage of new chances before they become popular can profit greatly. In the competition to create wealth, speed is a critical advantage, whether it is through new business model development, investing in burgeoning industries, or anticipating trends before they become popular.

Increasing Time Effectiveness

Since time is a limited resource, you lose out on more possibilities the longer it takes you to reach your financial objectives. With speed, you can make the most of your time and turn every second into a valuable opportunity to accumulate wealth. Your wealth-building endeavours can be expedited, allowing you to do more in less time and eventually meet your objectives earlier.

Welcoming Adaptability and Agility

People who can't adapt will inevitably fall behind as the financial landscape is ever-evolving. Maintaining agility and responsiveness in the face of disruptive technology, evolving trends, and changing market situations requires speed. You may swiftly adjust your tactics, seize new chances, and confidently ride the market's ups and downs by embracing the demand for speed.

Promoting an Innovative Culture

Being fast isn't the only aspect of speed; it also involves promoting an innovative and creative culture. Fostering an environment that values innovation and constant improvement can help you find new opportunities to provide value, open up undiscovered markets, even upend entire sectors. Innovation serves as the engine that accelerates progress and helps you reach your financial objectives in the fast lane of wealth growth.

The Fast lane Advantage: Using Speed to Your Advantage

Overcoming Time's Restraints

Time is frequently viewed in the conventional paradigm of wealth development as a challenge to be conquered and as a finite resource that needs to be properly budgeted and managed. But in the Fast lane, time turns from an enemy to a formidable friend. Through the use of velocity, or the rate at which wealth-building endeavours can be expedited, you can transcend temporal limitations and condense decades of advancement into a much shorter amount of time.

FASTLANE FORTUNE

Quickening the Creation of Wealth

The key to the Fast lane advantage is being able to quickly ramp up your efforts to accumulate riches. By utilizing the power of velocity, the Fast lane provides a shortcut to financial success while traditional techniques of saving and investing may only provide moderate and steady development over time. In a fraction of the time it would take using conventional methods, the Fast lane enables you to earn exponential gains through entrepreneurship, high-yield investments, or strategic leveraging.

Agilely Seizing Opportunities

Opportunities in the quick-changing world of wealth generation come and go in an instant. Your ability to act quickly and decisively to take advantage of these possibilities will give you the Fast lane advantage. Being quick is crucial for staying ahead of the curve and seizing chances before they pass you by, whether you're establishing a new company endeavour, identifying rising trends, or taking advantage of market inefficiencies.

Building Wealth at Your Pace

FASTLANE FORTUNE

Having the freedom to build money at your own pace is possibly the biggest benefit of the Fast lane strategy. With the Fast lane, you can take charge of your financial future and create an abundant and fulfilling life on your own terms, without having to wait decades to reach financial freedom through slow and steady savings. The Fast lane gives you the freedom and flexibility to live life on your terms, whether that means exploring the world, following your passions, or contributing to causes close to your heart.

Creating an Impactful Legacy

The Fast lane advantage goes beyond generating personal riches to include leaving a lasting legacy of influence and effect. By reaching financial success more quickly, you can use your resources and knowledge to change the world for the better. Through social entrepreneurship, mentoring, or philanthropy, the Fast lane enables you to make a lasting impact that goes well beyond your personal financial gain.

Decoding Exponential Development

Velocity in the Fast lane is about unlocking exponential growth, not just about speed. You may multiply your wealth more quickly by using the power of velocity, accomplishing in a matter of years what it could take others decades to do. With this exponential growth curve, you can quickly accumulate a sizeable nest egg and become financially independent in a short amount of time.

Beating Economic Uncertainty and Inflation

It may be difficult for the conventional method of wealth development to keep up with the rapid changes in the modern economy. It might not be possible to outpace inflation or shield your money from unstable economic conditions with slow and consistent development. The Fast lane advantage is its capacity to produce returns that significantly exceed inflation and act as a buffer against fluctuations in the economy. You may stay ahead of the curve and protect your financial future from unanticipated threats by utilizing velocity.

Generating Several Revenue Sources

The Fast lane approach's emphasis on generating various revenue streams is one of its main advantages. The Fast lane enables you to diversify your income streams and increase your resilience against job loss or market downturns rather than depending entirely on a single source of income, such as a salary or a traditional investment portfolio. With the Fast lane, you can generate a stable and secure income stream over time by building a portfolio of income-producing assets, whether through real estate investing, entrepreneurship, or other high-yield ventures.

Leaving the 9–5 grind behind

The typical 9–5 grind is a source of annoyance and discontent for a lot of individuals. The Fast lane provides an alternate route that enables you to create a lifestyle that is in line with your values and passions while escaping the confines of the conventional employment model. The Fast lane gives you the freedom to take back your time and live your life as you see fit, whether that means following your passion for entrepreneurship, seeing the world, or spending more time with loved ones.

Enhancing Wealth Across Generations

The Fast lane advantage goes beyond achieving individual financial success to include generating wealth across generations and leaving a durable legacy for future generations. You may guarantee a better future for your children and grandkids by using velocity to quickly amass wealth and provide them the means to prosper for many years to come. Whether it's through generosity, business, or smart estate planning, the Fast lane enables you to leave a lasting legacy that goes well beyond your own life.

FASTLANE FORTUNE

CHAPTER 2

Building Your Wealth Vehicle

Announcing Your Route to Wealth

Here is where the Fast lane trip really begins: creating your wealth vehicle. The fundamental techniques and procedures for locating and assembling the ideal wealth-building machine that will take you to financial independence and plenty will be covered in this chapter.

Locating Lucrative Prospects

Finding successful prospects in the market is the first stage in creating your wealth vehicle. This calls for in-depth study, trend analysis of the market, and identification of high demand and low competition sectors. Identifying chances that fit your interests, talents, and resources is essential whether it's a specialised business concept, a profitable investment opportunity, or a prospective real estate endeavour.

Market Potential and Demand Evaluation

Evaluating their market potential and demand comes next after you've found possible prospects. This includes researching the market, examining client demographics, and determining if your selected niche is viable. Knowing the wants and tastes of your target market can help you design your wealth vehicle to satisfy them and increase your chances of success.

The Fast lane Path You Choose

FASTLANE FORTUNE

With so many possible ways to create riches, you must select the Fast lane route that best fits your objectives. Investing, starting your own business, or doing both at once—the secret is to go down a route that plays to your interests, talents, and morals. You can position yourself for success and quicken your path to financial independence by choosing the ideal wealth vehicle.

Launching Your Wealth Vehicle

Having selected your wealth vehicle, it's time to roll up your sleeves and start to work. This can be starting a brand-new company, making wise investments, or buying assets that will bring in money. What ever route you select, the important thing is to move and begin gathering steam in the direction of your financial objectives. With the right goals, a well-thought-out strategy, and prompt action, you can transform your wealth vehicle into a potent force for wealth growth.

Welcoming Creativity and Flexibility

To keep ahead of the curve in the fast-paced world of wealth development, creativity and flexibility are necessity. As you construct your wealth vehicle, keep yourself receptive to fresh concepts, tools, and tactics that can provide you an advantage over competitors. Staying flexible and change-responsive is essential whether implementing new business models, capitalizing on new trends, or embracing disruptive technologies.

Selecting Lucrative Prospects

An Analysis of Market Dynamics

Having a thorough understanding of market dynamics is the first step towards achieving financial independence. The first step in creating wealth, be it through investing, business, or other pursuits, is to research the various opportunities that are open to you. This entails carrying out in-depth market research, examining market trends, and pinpointing regions with strong demand and little competition.

Determining Pain Points and Unmet Needs

Every lucrative opportunity starts with an unmet need or pain point that has to be addressed. Determining chances that provide real value to your target market is crucial, regardless of whether the product or service addresses a prevalent issue, simplifies a laborious procedure, or satisfies an unfulfilled need. Understanding your clients' requirements and problems might help you find profitable possibilities with the potential to yield sizable returns.

Evaluating Market Growth and Potential

Examining possible possibilities' market potential and growth

prospects comes next after you've identified them. This entails assessing the competitive landscape, market size, and growth trends to ascertain whether your selected niche is viable. You can acquire insights into the possible risks and rewards associated with various prospects and make well-informed judgements about where to spend your time and money by carrying out in-depth market research and due diligence.

Investigating Up-and-Coming Trends and Technologies

The opportunities landscape in today's fast-paced world is always changing. Exploring new trends and technologies that have the potential to upend sectors and open up new avenues for wealth creation is crucial to staying ahead of the curve. Whether it's the development of artificial intelligence, the growing acceptance of sustainable investing, or the introduction of new consumer trends, staying abreast of these developments and positioning yourself to take advantage of new opportunities are crucial.

Carrying Out Competition Research

To comprehend the competitive landscape and spot gaps and opportunities in the market, competitor analysis is just as crucial as investigating market dynamics and trends. This entails investigating rival goods and services, evaluating their advantages and disadvantages, and figuring out how to set yourself apart from the competition and provide a special value proposition to your intended audience.

Comprehending the Pain Points of Customers

Successful ventures and investments frequently result from meeting critical demands or resolving major client pain points. Take the time to thoroughly comprehend the problems, aspirations, and frustrations of your target audience. Through identifying with their experiences, you might find profitable opportunities that truly bring value and fill gaps in the market.

A Study of Niche Markets

Niche markets present a plethora of options for investors and entrepreneurs in the connected world of today. Think about markets that are underserved or have specialised needs as an alternative to competing in oversaturated markets. Investigate markets or communities where you have specialised knowledge or interests to help you build out a successful niche and position yourself as a leader in your industry.

Identifying Disruptions and Trends

Keeping up with new developments and trends can reveal profitable chances to build money. Keep an eye on changes in consumer behaviour, technology developments, legislative actions, and worldwide market trends. You may get ahead of the curve and profit from shifting market dynamics by projecting future needs and making early adjustments to shifting environments.

Evaluating Social and Economic Factors

The business environment is shaped by the interaction of social and economic factors, which offers chances for savvy investors and businesspeople. Examine demographic changes, financial trends, and geopolitical developments to determine which industries are most likely to grow or experience upheaval. Aligning your endeavours with dominant social and economic forces will help you overcome obstacles and surf the waves of fortune.

Using Analytics and Data

In the era of big data, strategic decision-making can be aided by utilising analytics and data-driven insights to find untapped opportunities. Utilise consumer surveys, market research, and predictive analytics to gather useful information on consumer preferences, market demand, and rivalry. You may minimise risks and increase your chances of success by basing your judgements on scientific evidence.

Collaboration and networking

Building relationships and working together within your professional network can lead to opportunities. Interact with mentors, thought leaders, and colleagues in the business to share insights, brainstorm, and find possible joint ventures or funding sources. You can broaden your horizons in terms of wealth-building and gain access to new opportunities by cultivating meaningful relationships and utilising pooled skills.

FASTLANE FORTUNE

Assessing Demand and Market Potential

Evaluating Market Growth and Size

Analysing the market's size and growth trajectory is one of the first steps in assessing its potential. Look for information on the overall demand for a good or service within a certain market sector, often known as the total addressable market (TAM). Assess past growth rates and projections to determine the market's potential for growth. A market that is big and expanding means there are lots of chances for wealth generation and scalability.

Knowing the Needs and Preferences of the Customer

It's critical to comprehend the requirements, preferences, and pain points of your target market in order to correctly estimate market demand. To learn more about the tastes and behaviours of your customers, do focus groups, surveys, and market research. Determine which underserved market niches or unmet demands your product or service may significantly improve. You may more successfully take advantage of market opportunities if your offers are in line with what customers want.

Evaluating the Competitive Environment

FASTLANE FORTUNE

It is essential to analyse the competitive environment in order to comprehend market dynamics and properly position your offerings. Determine the main rivals' advantages, disadvantages, and market share. Analyse their distribution networks, price policies, and range of products. Seek out opportunities to distinguish your offerings and obtain a competitive edge by looking for underserved or gaps in the market. You might find chances to carve out your niche and take market share by doing a thorough competitor analysis.

Examining Market Drivers and Trends

Demand is shaped by market trends and drivers, which also provide up potential for wealth development. To spot new opportunities and risks, keep an eye on consumer preferences, technological developments, industry trends, and regulatory changes. Seek out trends that fit your interests, skills, and areas of strength. You may put yourself in a successful position in industries that are changing quickly by staying ahead of the curve and making adjustments for shifting market dynamics.

Evaluating Entry Barriers

FASTLANE FORTUNE

Analyse the obstacles to entrance in your chosen market, including the level of competition, capital needs, and regulatory requirements. High entry barriers can reduce competition and provide market leaders the chance to seize share and make steady profits. Low entry barriers, on the other hand, could result in fierce rivalry and pressure on prices. Understanding the competitive environment and entrance barriers can help you determine whether it's feasible to enter a certain market and create effective methods to deal with obstacles.

Projecting Demand and Potential Revenue

Forecast demand and income potential for your offerings based on your understanding of the market. To forecast future sales and revenue, calculate pricing elasticity, adoption curves, and market penetration rates. To account for uncertainties and reduce risks, take into consideration a variety of scenarios and sensitivity studies. You may increase your chances of success by setting realistic goals and allocating resources wisely by creating realistic revenue estimates.

Evaluating Target Market Divide

Knowing how your target market is segmented is essential to doing an effective market analysis. Determine different client segments according to behavioural traits, psychographics, and demographics. Determine the size, potential for growth, and purchasing power of each group to help you focus your marketing efforts and customise your products to fit their needs. You can increase your chances of success and obtain a competitive edge by focusing on niche markets with unmet requirements and strong development potential.

Evaluating Consumer Trends and Behaviour

The dynamic nature of consumer behaviour is attributed to shifting lifestyles, socioeconomic variables, and tastes. Keep an eye out for changes in consumer behaviour, such as the emergence of e-commerce, dietary habits, or a growth in the desire for environmentally friendly products. Examine customer patterns and cultural factors to predict future needs and modify your products appropriately. You may maintain your lead and increase your market share by matching your goods and services to changing consumer tastes.

Evaluating Legal and Regulatory Considerations

Legal and regulatory issues have the power to drastically alter market dynamics and erect obstacles to entry for new competitors. To determine if entering the business is feasible, evaluate the legal requirements, licencing processes, and compliance standards in your target market. Examine the effects of regulatory modifications on market demand and competitive dynamics, such as new laws or industry rules. You may minimise risks, guarantee compliance, and take advantage of market opportunities by comprehending and managing the intricacies of regulations.

Performing a SWOT evaluation

To assess market potential and demand, a SWOT analysis (Strengths, Weaknesses, Opportunities, Threats) is a useful tool. Evaluate your advantages and disadvantages in addition to outside chances and dangers in the marketplace. Determine the main market forces, your competitors' advantages, and any possible risks to your venture or investment plan. You may improve your chances of success by making well-informed judgements and gaining a deeper grasp of the market landscape by performing a thorough SWOT analysis.

Using Data Analytics and Market Research

Data analytics and market research offer insightful information about customer preferences, competitive dynamics, and market trends. Use both quantitative and qualitative research techniques, such as data analysis, focus groups, and surveys, to obtain useful information and corroborate your hypotheses. To predict demand, spot new opportunities, and enhance your marketing tactics, use data-driven methods. In quickly changing marketplaces, you can remain ahead of the competition and make well-informed decisions by utilising market research and data analytics.

Looking for Approval and Input

Lastly, to validate your company and market ideas, ask respected advisors, industry insiders, and future clients for their opinions and confirmation. To gain feedback and improve your services, ask target customers through pilot programmes, product prototypes, or beta testing. Interact with colleagues in the field, mentors, and advisers to obtain insightful opinions and insights about market trends and opportunities. You may improve your approach and raise your chances of success in the market by adding validation and feedback into your market analysis process.

FASTLANE FORTUNE

Selecting Your Fastlane Route: Investing, Business, or Both?

Knowing Your Objectives and Preferences

To select your Fastlane course, you must first determine your objectives, inclinations, and level of risk tolerance. Whichever route best fits your desired outcomes will depend on your long-term goals, financial targets, and personal values. Do you have a stronger desire to start a business from the ground up or do you think that investment portfolios with stability and diversity are preferable? You may choose the best Fastlane course for you by being clear about your preferences and ambitions.

A Look into Entrepreneurship

The ability to start something from nothing and develop creative concepts into successful businesses is what entrepreneurship gives. If you're a risk-taker, love to solve issues, and thrive in dynamic surroundings, becoming an entrepreneur could be the best Fastlane career choice for you. Starting your own business gives you the freedom to follow your passions, let your creativity run wild, and create money at your own pace—whether you're starting a local

FASTLANE FORTUNE

company, a tech startup, or an internet endeavour.

Acknowledging Investments

Investing offers a different way to build wealth by giving you the chance to increase your capital through asset management and wise allocation. Investing might be the best Fast lane option for you if you'd rather take a more laissez-faire approach to accumulating wealth. Investments, whether they be in stocks, bonds, real estate, or other alternative assets, let you diversify your holdings, earn passive income, and amass wealth over time. Financial independence can be attained without the daily responsibilities of managing a business by conducting thorough research and adhering to strict investing practices.

Taking a Look at Hybrid Methods

A lot of people decide to take a hybrid approach, mixing aspects of investments and entrepreneurship to maximise wealth-building potential and diversify their sources of income. This could be working a full-time job and beginning a side business, investing business revenues in stocks or real estate, or using your entrepreneurial abilities to spot and seize profitable investment possibilities. By using a hybrid strategy, you can minimise risks and maximise profits while taking use of the advantages of both investing and entrepreneurship.

Evaluating Risk and Benefit

Whichever Fast lane route you decide on, you must carefully weigh the risks and benefits involved. Higher levels of risk, uncertainty, and volatility are frequently associated with entrepreneurship; there is a chance of failure in addition to the possibility of huge gains. Contrarily, investments provide a more dependable and varied method of accumulating wealth, however they might not produce as high of returns as profitable business endeavours. When assessing the risk-reward profile of each Fast lane course, take your time horizon, financial resources, and risk tolerance into account.

According to Your Proficiency and Knowledge

In the end, the fastest route should match your interests, talents, and areas of competence. When deciding between investing and entrepreneurship, take into account your expertise, industry knowledge, and strengths. Entrepreneurship can be a good fit for you if you have experience in marketing, product development, or business management. Investing can be a better fit if you possess a talent for risk management, portfolio diversification, or financial research. Your chances of success in the Fast lane of wealth creation can be increased by making the most of your abilities and knowledge.

Investigating the Entrepreneurial Path

Becoming an entrepreneur is a journey full with obstacles, victories, and priceless lessons. Beyond the possibility of financial gain, becoming an entrepreneur gives you the chance to follow your passions, have a significant effect, and leave a lasting legacy. Entrepreneurship can be the ideal Fast lane career option for you if you enjoy being creative, taking measured chances, and leading with vision. Entrepreneurship gives you the freedom to choose your own path and shape the future you want, whether you're drawn to the joy of creating something from scratch, the excitement of starting a startup, or the independence of being your own boss.

Entry into the Investing World

Compared to entrepreneurship, investments offer a route to wealth growth that requires less management and active participation. By strategically allocating your funds among a variety of asset types,

FASTLANE FORTUNE

including stocks, bonds, real estate, and alternative investments, investing enables you to increase your financial resources. Investing offers the flexibility to diversify your portfolio, create passive income, and gradually increase your wealth if you want a more laissez-faire approach to wealth development. You may build a safe financial future for yourself and your loved ones and attain financial freedom with disciplined investing methods and a long-term outlook.

Weighting Risk and Benefit

A crucial factor to take into account when selecting your Fast lane course is striking a balance between risk and profit. Compared to investing, entrepreneurship frequently involves higher levels of risk, uncertainty, and volatility. Successful business endeavours include a risk of failure and financial loss, but they can also result in considerable rewards and personal fulfilment. In contrast, investments provide a more dependable and varied method of accumulating money, although they might not produce as high of returns as profitable ventures. In order to select a Fast lane option that best suits your situation in terms of risk and reward, take into account your time horizon, financial resources, and risk tolerance.

Examining Diversification and Hybrid Models

FASTLANE FORTUNE

A lot of people decide to take a hybrid strategy to building wealth, mixing aspects of investing and entrepreneurship to maximise returns and diversify their sources of income. This might be launching a business and making concurrent investments in stocks, real estate, or other assets in order to distribute risk and take advantage of opportunities to accumulate wealth. By using a hybrid strategy, you can minimise risks and maximise profits while taking use of the advantages of both investing and entrepreneurship. A stable and resilient portfolio can be created by diversifying among a variety of asset classes and income sources, even in the face of market and economic volatility.

Taking Personal Preferences and Lifestyle Into Account

In the end, the best Fast lane route is the one that fits your long-term objectives, lifestyle, and personal tastes. Think about things like autonomy, flexibility, and work-life balance when deciding between investing and starting your own business. Being an entrepreneur may provide you the flexibility to follow your hobbies, make your own hours, and design a fulfilling and independent lifestyle. However, without the obligations of managing a business, investments may offer the freedom to make passive income, travel, or spend time with loved ones. You may

FASTLANE FORTUNE

design a rewarding and long-lasting strategy for wealth building that enhances your general well-being and pleasure by matching your Fast lane path with your preferences and way of life.

CHAPTER 3

Leverage to Accelerate Wealth

Comprehending the Leverage Power

Leverage is an effective financial strategy that you may use to increase the returns on your investments and hasten the process of building wealth. Leverage is essentially the use of borrowed funds to raise the possible rate of return on investment. Through the process of leveraging your current assets, equity, or cash, you can increase your purchasing power and take advantage of possibilities that might not otherwise be available to you. Leverage offers a road to exponential wealth growth, whether it is used to buy stocks using margin accounts, invest in real estate with borrowed funds, or use financial derivatives to increase profits.

Leverage Types

Leverage comes in a variety of forms, each with advantages, disadvantages, and consequences of their own:

1. Financial Leverage: Investing in income-producing assets like stocks or real estate requires borrowing money. By leveraging

borrowed money to enhance your investment exposure, this type of leverage enables you to increase your returns. Financial leverage can increase profits, but it can also increase losses and increase the danger of financial instability if it is not used carefully.

2. Operational Leverage : To increase profits, operational leverage entails making your business processes more productive and efficient. You can expand your business's operations and increase profitability by optimising resources, streamlining procedures, and scaling your business. With operational leverage, you may increase revenue per unit of input, which raises margins and speeds up wealth accumulation.

3. Strategic Leverage : To obtain a competitive edge and spur growth, strategic leverage entails making use of strategic alliances, partnerships, and resources. Through strategic asset acquisition, market expansion, or joint ventures with like-minded companies, you can make better use of outside resources to strengthen your competitive edge and reach a wider audience. By using strategic leverage, you can increase your resources and capabilities and hasten the production of wealth and prosperity.

Advantages of Utilisation

Leverage provides numerous important advantages for generating money.

1. Amplified Returns : Leverage allows you to increase wealth growth and investment returns. Because leveraged investments let you control greater positions with a smaller initial investment, they have the potential to yield more profits than unleveraged investments.

2. Diversification : By spreading risk among a number of different assets or asset classes, leverage enables you to diversify your investing portfolio. You can lessen your exposure to any one asset or market and improve the overall resilience of your portfolio by spreading your wealth across a variety of investments.

3. **Access to Opportunities**: By using leverage, one can take advantage of opportunities that would not otherwise be possible. Investing in high-yield assets or profitable companies with borrowed cash allows you to take advantage of growth and wealth development opportunities that might not be accessible through conventional means.

FASTLANE FORTUNE

4. **Flexibility**: You may manage your assets and use your capital in a flexible way when you use leverage. Leverage gives you the financial freedom to carry out your strategic objectives and meet your wealth-building targets, whether you're trying to grow your company operations, diversify your investments, or take on new projects.

Thoughts and Dangers

Leverage has some inherent risks and considerations, even though it can speed up wealth creation:

1. **Financial Risk**: Capital loss and unstable finances are more likely with leveraged investments since they amplify wins and losses. Significant financial risk can result from high levels of leverage, particularly in erratic or turbulent markets.

2. **Interest Costs**: Interest expenses incurred when borrowing money for investments can lower profitability and degrade investment returns. It's critical to compare the possible returns against the costs of borrowing and to carefully consider the cost of leverage.

3. **Market Volatility**: Because leveraged investments increase

the effect of price movements on investment returns, they are more susceptible to market swings and volatility. Margin calls and significant losses can result from market downturns, particularly if leverage is employed excessively or without appropriate risk management.

4. **Liquidity Constraints** : In order to satisfy margin calls or debt obligations, leveraged investments may need continuous capital commitments and liquidity. It's critical to keep enough cash on hand and financial reserves to handle unforeseen costs and any liquidity restrictions.

Effective Leverage Strategies

In order to efficiently leverage and reduce potential hazards, take into account these tactics:

1. **Risk Management**: To lessen the possible negative effects of leverage, put strong risk management techniques into place. To prevent losses and safeguard wealth, implement stop-loss orders, diversify your investment portfolio, and set stringent risk limits.

2. **Discipline and Patience**: Refrain from making snap judgements or taking unwarranted risks while utilising leverage.

FASTLANE FORTUNE

Instead, use discipline and patience. Adhere to your investing strategy, keep an eye towards the long term, and refrain from pursuing quick profits at the price of stability over the long run.

3. **Due Diligence** : Before using your funds, do out extensive research and due diligence and carefully weigh the possible benefits and dangers of each investment opportunity. To make wise investment selections, assess the reliability of counterparties, the quality of assets, and the strength of the underlying fundamentals.

4. **Stress Testing**: To evaluate the resilience and potential vulnerabilities of your investment portfolio and leverage positions, stress-test them under various market situations. To reduce downside risk, think about how your investments might fare in a down market and modify your leverage levels appropriately.

Examples & Case Studies

Many prosperous businesspeople and investors have used leverage to quicken the accumulation of wealth:

1. **Real Estate Investors**: Real estate investors frequently use leverage to finance the majority of a property's cost with a

mortgage and make only a small down payment. They can increase their returns through rental revenue and property appreciation by using leverage on their initial investment.

2. **Hedge Fund Managers**: Leverage is a tool used by hedge fund managers to increase returns and compound investment gains. Hedge funds can increase the size of their investment strategies and increase returns for their investors by utilising leverage through margin trading, derivatives, or leveraged ETFs.

3. **Entrepreneurs**: To build their companies quickly and scale them, entrepreneurs make use of their resources, knowledge, and abilities. Businesses can expand faster and get a larger market share by utilising external capital, strategic alliances, and operational savings.

Making Use of Intellectual Capital

Intellectual capital can be used in conjunction with financial resources to speed up the production of riches. By utilising their knowledge, abilities, and experience, investors and entrepreneurs may spot profitable possibilities, come up with creative solutions, and add value to the market. Individuals can obtain a competitive edge, set themselves apart from rivals, and produce long-term, sustainable growth by utilising intellectual capital. Intellectual capital may be a potent tool for generating wealth and succeeding in the fast lane, whether by building a strong personal brand, creating innovative technologies, or pioneering ground-breaking research.

Using Leverage to Make Strategic Decisions

Effective leverage is not limited to financial transactions; it also includes resource allocation and strategic decision-making. People may make well-informed judgements and maximise returns on a variety of business and investment ventures by utilising data analytics, market insights, and predictive modelling. Making use of cutting-edge technology like machine learning and artificial intelligence can boost productivity, spur innovation, and improve decision-making processes. In the Fast lane of wealth creation, people can optimise profits, reduce risks, and attain better outcomes by incorporating leverage into their strategic decision-making.

Using Network Effects to Their Full Potential

Through the use of network effects, wealth development can be accelerated by utilising the strength of interdependent relationships and cooperative ecosystems. People can get significant resources, opportunities, and support networks by developing strong networks, meaningful relationships, and strategic collaborations. By taking use of network effects, people can increase their impact, broaden their audience, and seize fresh growth prospects. People can use network effects to quicken their path to financial independence and success in the Fastlane, whether through industry groups, online communities, or networking events.

Maximising Utilisation in Various Aspects

Optimising leverage across a variety of dimensions—financial, operational, intellectual, and relational—is necessary for effective leveraging. Individuals can maximise their potential for developing wealth and create sustainable long-term growth by embracing a holistic approach to leverage. In order to do this, one may need to use network effects to create cooperative relationships, intellectual capital to generate creative ideas, or financial resources to invest in operational improvements. In the Fast lane of wealth creation, people can forge partnerships, reduce risks, and seize chances for exponential growth by optimising leverage across several dimensions.

Switching with the Dynamics of the Market

Adaptability and agility are necessary for effective leveraging in a dynamic and changing market environment. People need to keep an eye on market trends, evaluate the competitive landscape, and modify their leverage techniques as needed. Through constant observation and adaptation to shifting market circumstances, people may take advantage of new opportunities, reduce risks, and maintain a competitive edge. To effectively leverage and achieve sustained wealth creation in the Fastlane, one must adapt to shifting market conditions, whether through innovation-driven techniques, diversification initiatives, or strategic pivot plans.

Controlling Hazards and Safeguarding Funds

Leverage has the potential to increase wealth development, but it also has risks that need to be properly considered, controlled, and reduced. Strong risk management techniques must be put in place by individuals in order to safeguard their money and reduce any losses. This could entail diversifying investment portfolios, imposing stringent risk limitations, and keeping enough cash on hand to pay for unforeseen costs. In the face of market volatility and uncertainty, people may protect their money and guarantee long-term financial security by placing a high priority on capital preservation and risk mitigation.

FASTLANE FORTUNE

Examples & Case Studies

Many prosperous people and businesses have achieved amazing wealth creation by skillfully utilising their networks, resources, and expertise:

1. Tech Entrepreneurs : To develop and grow cutting-edge companies like Google, Facebook, and Amazon, Silicon Valley entrepreneurs have made use of their technological know-how, industry connections, and venture capital backing. In a comparatively short amount of time, these tech entrepreneurs have revolutionised markets, changed industries, and made enormous fortune by utilising network effects, intellectual capital, and strategic collaborations.

2. Real Estate Moguls : To create enormous real estate empires, real estate moguls like Sam Zell and Donald Trump have made strategic acquisitions, used their financial clout, and gained market expertise. These real estate tycoons have accumulated substantial fortune and left long legacies in the real estate sector by utilising financial leverage, operational efficiencies, and market insights.

3. Investment Gurus : Renowned investors such as George Soros

and Warren Buffett have achieved remarkable returns in the financial markets by utilising their disciplined approaches, long-term outlook, and investment acumen. These investing gurus have regularly outperformed the market and made significant wealth for themselves and their investors by utilising contrarian strategies, fundamental analysis, and patient capital.

FASTLANE FORTUNE

Making Assets Work for You: Leveraging Systems**

Awareness of Systems Thinking

Understanding the relationships between different parts of a complex system and how they interact to achieve particular results is known as systems thinking. Systems thinking in the context of wealth creation is creating, putting into place, and refining systems that produce passive revenue, simplify procedures, and add value with little continuous work. People can find leverage points, maximise productivity, and greatly expand their wealth-building endeavours by embracing a systems thinking mentality.

Creating Scalable Architectures

Over time, scalable systems enable people to boost productivity, reach a wider audience, and earn passive money since they are built to grow and adapt to changing demands. Scalable systems use technology, automation, and outsourcing to reduce manual intervention and increase productivity. Examples of these systems include automated e-commerce platforms, digital courses, and subscription-based services. People can construct assets that work for them 24/7, creating passive income and accumulating wealth even while they sleep, by designing scalable systems.

Streamlining Revenue Streams

Leveraging systems for wealth generation requires automation, which enables people to automate income streams and lessen their dependency on active participation. This could be putting in place email marketing campaigns, digital product delivery platforms, or automated sales funnels that require little upkeep and create passive income. People can focus on higher-value tasks that promote growth and innovation, free up time, and eliminate manual labour by utilising automation techniques and technology.

Delegating Non-Corrective Work

Another tactic for maximising efficiency and utilising systems is to outsource non-essential work. People can free up time, energy, and resources to concentrate on strategic objectives and core business activities by assigning low-value or routine duties to outside service providers. Through the use of freelancers, specialised agencies, or virtual assistants, outsourcing enables people to take use of outside knowledge, grow their businesses, and create money more quickly while retaining flexibility and agility.

Putting Passive Investment Strategies Into Practice

FASTLANE FORTUNE

Investing in assets or vehicles that produce appreciation and passive income over time, such as dividend-paying stocks, rental properties, or index funds, is known as passive investment techniques. Through the use of passive investment strategies, people can diversify their portfolio, take advantage of compound interest, and accumulate long-term wealth with little to no effort on their part. A hands-off approach to wealth creation is provided by passive investments, which enable people to grow their money and generate income while concentrating on other goals or priorities.

Streamlining Procedures for Effectiveness

In order to maximise returns on investment and leverage systems efficiently, efficiency is essential. To increase productivity and efficiency, people should always be streamlining workflows, getting rid of bottlenecks, and optimising procedures. This could entail using lean techniques, using best practices, or utilising technology to reduce waste and increase productivity. Through process optimisation for efficiency, people can increase profits, save expenses, and create wealth more quickly in a variety of company and investment ventures.

Evaluating Output and Continuing

FASTLANE FORTUNE

Leveraging systems effectively and attaining long-term, sustainable growth require constant improvement. To find areas for optimisation and improvement, people should routinely measure performance, monitor important metrics, and evaluate the outcomes. Through data collection, feedback, and strategy iteration, people can improve the efficacy of their systems and adjust to the ever-changing dynamics of the market. Individuals can stay ahead of the curve and spur innovation in the Fastlane of wealth creation by adopting a culture of constant improvement.

Examples & Case Studies

Many prosperous people and businesses have successfully used systems to generate assets that benefit them:

1. Digital Entrepreneurs : To build wealth and attain financial independence, digital entrepreneurs like Pat Flynn and Tim Ferriss have used automated sales funnels, scalable web platforms, and passive income streams. Through their creation of membership sites, digital products, and online courses, these entrepreneurs have developed scalable systems that add value for their audiences while producing passive revenue.

FASTLANE FORTUNE

2. Real Estate Investors : Real estate investors use rental revenue streams, property management systems, and passive investment techniques to build wealth via real estate syndications and rental properties. Real estate investors can create long-term wealth in the real estate market by putting in place effective property management systems, contracting out maintenance, and taking advantage of property appreciation.

3. Index Fund Investors : To create diversified portfolios and accomplish long-term wealth creation, passive investors make use of index funds, exchange-traded funds (ETFs), and other passive investment vehicles. Passive investors can take advantage of compounding gains, cut costs, and eventually attain market-like returns by investing in inexpensive, diversified index funds that mimic broad market indices.

Creating assets that work for you, earning passive income, and expediting wealth growth in the Fast lane may all be achieved by utilising systems. Through the use of scalable internet platforms, automated revenue streams, or passive investment strategies, people can focus on higher-value activities that foster growth and innovation while maximising efficiency and reducing physical labour. People can establish scalable assets that produce passive income and long-term value in the Fast lane of wealth creation by

FASTLANE FORTUNE

embracing continuous improvement, optimising procedures, and adopting a systems thinking mentality.

Using Other People's Resources: Money, Time, and Knowledge

Comprehending the Leverage Power

A key idea in wealth creation is leverage, which enables people to pool their resources and exert more effort to produce bigger and better outcomes than they might otherwise. Using other people's resources—including their time, money, and expertise—is essential to optimising wealth generation. Through the use of outside resources, people can more efficiently scale their commercial endeavours, investments, and projects by gaining access to more money, knowledge, and labour.

Making Use of Other People's Time

People's time is one of the most valuable resources that people may use. By assigning responsibilities to others, hiring staff, or outsourcing projects, people can take use of the time and abilities of others to complete more work in less time. It is possible for people to concentrate on higher-priority tasks that call for their specialised knowledge and attention when they delegate regular or low-value chores. Using other people's time allows businesses to develop faster, boost efficiency, and scale operations through the hiring of workers, freelancers, or virtual assistants.

Using Money Belonging to Others

Having access to other people's funds is yet another effective leverage strategy for generating riches. Individuals can utilise external cash to finance business ventures, real estate investments, or entrepreneurial endeavours, either by borrowing, crowdfunding, or investment capital seeking. People can overcome capital limitations, explore growth opportunities, and increase returns on investment by gaining access to other people's money. By utilising other people's money, one can more quickly expand their wealth-building endeavours and make more use of outside resources, such as venture capital, business loans, and partnerships.

Using the Experience of Others

People can take advantage of other people's knowledge to reduce risks, quicken their learning curve, and produce better outcomes in addition to saving time and money. People can obtain insights, access opportunities, and steer clear of costly mistakes by drawing on the knowledge, experience, and networks of specialists in their area through mentorship, advisory boards, or strategic alliances. People can establish more successful tactics, make better decisions, and confidently handle difficult situations by utilising the expertise of others.

Forging Strategic Alliances

Strategic alliances are an effective means of taking advantage of the knowledge, connections, and resources of others for your own gain. People can access more resources, reach a wider audience, and develop synergies that spur growth and innovation by forming alliances with companies that complement their own, with colleagues in the sector, or with strategic investors. Creating strategic partnerships, whether they be joint ventures, co-branding campaigns, or strategic alliances, enables people to take advantage of outside resources and skills to meet goals and expedite wealth generation.

Delegating and Empowering

FASTLANE FORTUNE

Using other people's time, money, and talent efficiently requires empowerment and responsibility delegation. People can use their abilities and skills to better accomplish shared objectives by giving teammates, collaborators, or partners the freedom to take on jobs and initiatives. People can take use of the combined knowledge and inventiveness of their groups by delegating authority and decision-making, which helps them come up with new ideas, solve problems, and carry out tasks more successfully and efficiently.

Building Win-Win Connections

Establishing win-win partnerships is the cornerstone of effectively using the time, resources, and knowledge of others. Through incentive alignment, risk and reward sharing, and teamwork, people may build win-win relationships that generate value for all stakeholders. In the Fastlane of wealth creation, building win-win connections promotes trust, loyalty, and long-term success through the provision of value-added services, equity shares, or income stream sharing.

Examples & Case Studies

Many prosperous people and businesses have successfully used the resources of others—including their time, money, and expertise—

FASTLANE FORTUNE

to produce amazing outcomes:

1. Tech Entrepreneurs : To create cutting-edge businesses like Facebook and Tesla, tech entrepreneurs like Elon Musk and Mark Zuckerberg have benefited from venture capital financing, strategic alliances, and top personnel. These entrepreneurs have disrupted sectors, swiftly scaled their enterprises, and generated enormous value for shareholders by leveraging outside resources and skills.

2. **Real Estate Developers**: To fund significant development projects, real estate developers take advantage of other people's funds via joint ventures, bank loans, and private equity investments. Through collaboration with lenders, contractors, and investors, real estate developers can obtain the necessary funds, know-how, and assets to effectively purchase, develop, and oversee real estate.

3. **Small Business Owners**: To grow their operations and reach, small business owners make strategic alliances, hire staff, and outsource services, all of which allow them to take use of other

people's time. Small business owners can concentrate on growth efforts, innovation, and strategic decision-making that will lead to long-term success by assigning duties and responsibilities. .
Increasing Your Intensity: From Regional to Worldwide Effect**

FASTLANE FORTUNE

Comprehending the Scale Effect

A key idea in business and entrepreneurship is scale, which is the capacity to boost productivity, broaden influence, and multiply impact without correspondingly raising expenses or resources. Leveraging systems, technology, and strategic initiatives to reach a wider audience, break into new markets, and effect positive change globally are all part of scaling your efforts from local to global impact. Individuals and organisations may increase their impact, spur innovation, and change the world by utilising the power of scale.

Selecting Areas for Growth

Finding growth prospects and possibilities for expansion is the first step in scaling your activities. Finding growth prospects involves conducting market research, making strategic plans, and having a thorough grasp of the demands and preferences of customers. This is true whether one is looking to expand into new areas, introduce cutting-edge products, or diversify sources of income. Through comprehensive market analysis, consumer feedback collection, and competition dynamics evaluation, individuals and organisations can pinpoint unexplored prospects and formulate growth and expansion strategies.

Scalable Business Model Adoption

The development of scalable business models is necessary to move initiatives from local to global influence. Scalable business models, such as those found in software-as-a-service (SaaS) platforms, e-commerce sites, and subscription-based services, enable people and businesses to expand and adjust to shifting market conditions while reaching a wider clientele and producing steady, long-term income. Scalable business models let people and companies grow their operations successfully and efficiently by utilising technology, automation, and economies of scale.

FASTLANE FORTUNE

Increasing Market Capacity

A crucial element of growing initiatives from local to global impact is increasing market penetration. Individuals and organisations can reach new audiences and access new markets through digital marketing, strategic collaborations, or foreign growth in order to increase their impact and bring about positive change on a global scale. Through the utilisation of digital platforms, social media accounts, and online marketplaces, people and businesses may expand their global brand reach to millions of prospective clients throughout the globe.

Making Use of Innovation and Technology

Innovation and technology are strong accelerators of scale, enabling people and businesses to increase productivity, automate procedures, and seize new chances for development and expansion. People and organisations can use technology to improve customer experiences, expedite processes, and spur innovation at scale. Examples of this include using blockchain technology, artificial intelligence, and data analytics. A culture of innovation and keeping up with developing technology allow people and organisations to stay ahead of the curve and bring about disruptive change on a global scale.

Forging Strategic Alliances

Forming strategic alliances is crucial to increasing market penetration and scaling initiatives. In order to attain greater impact and expedite growth, people and organisations might collaborate with complementary firms, industry peers, or strategic investors to gain access to extra resources, experience, and networks. Through strategic partnerships, people and organisations may expand their efforts and bring about positive change on a global scale by utilising external assets and capabilities, whether through joint

FASTLANE FORTUNE

ventures, co-branding projects, or distribution agreements.

Evaluating Effect and Efficiency

Scaling activities and assessing results require measuring impact and effectiveness. To reach their objectives, people and organisations must evaluate progress, measure results, and make necessary adjustments to their strategies—whether through metrics, impact assessments, or key performance indicators (KPIs). Individuals and organisations can get insights into what's working, what isn't, and how to maximise their efforts for maximum impact and effectiveness by gathering data, analysing results, and asking stakeholders for feedback.

Examples & Case Studies

Many prosperous people and institutions have expanded their efforts from regional to worldwide influence:

1. **Social Entrepreneurs**: In order to solve global issues like poverty, education, and healthcare, social entrepreneurs like Muhammad Yunus, the creator of Grameen Bank, have increased the scope of their initiatives. Social entrepreneurs have the ability to develop solutions that are scalable and empower people and communities all over the world by utilising microfinance, social enterprises, and community-based initiatives.

2. **Tech companies**: By using technology, creativity, and smart alliances, tech companies like Airbnb and Uber have expanded their operations from a local to a worldwide influence. These firms have completely changed how people commute, travel, and access services all around the world by upending established industries and utilising the sharing economy.

3. **Nonprofit Organisations**: To address global challenges including healthcare, conservation, and humanitarian relief,

FASTLANE FORTUNE

nonprofits like World Wildlife Fund and Doctors Without Borders have increased the scope of their work. Nonprofit organisations can mobilise resources, generate awareness, and promote positive change globally by collaborating with governments, non-governmental organisations, and corporate sponsors.

CHAPTER 4

The Wealth Acceleration Commandments**

"The Commandments of Wealth Acceleration" are a set of guidelines for people who want to get richer and more financially independent faster. In the Fastlane of wealth growth, these commandments encompass crucial tactics, mentalities, and doable measures for attaining riches acceleration and building enduring prosperity.

1. You Will Adopt an Abundant Mindset

Adopting an attitude of abundance is the first wealth acceleration commandment. Develop an abundant mindset that acknowledges the limitless options and possibilities present in the universe, as opposed to giving in to limiting ideas or scarcity thinking. Adopt an attitude of thankfulness, optimism, and plenty, understanding that success and money are not limited resources but rather plentiful and available to people who see their own potential and act with inspiration.

2. You Must Establish Specific Goals and Objectives

The secret to accelerating riches is clarity. Establish definite, well-defined goals and objectives in line with your priorities, values, and vision. Make sure your wealth-building journey has direction and focus by setting SMART (Specific, Measurable, Achievable, Relevant, Time-bound) goals, which can help you achieve financial independence, start a profitable business, or generate passive income streams. Put your objectives down on paper, make strategies for how you'll get there, and make a commitment to acting with purpose and consistency.

3. You Will Make an Investment in Your Own Education and Personal Growth

To accelerate wealth accumulation, self-education and personal growth must be prioritised. Make a commitment to lifetime learning, ongoing development, and personal advancement in areas related to your wealth-building objectives. Whether it's developing your knowledge, gaining new abilities, or refining existing skills, spend money on books, classes, mentors, and experiences that will enable you to achieve new heights of fulfilment and success. Never forget that investing in yourself is the best investment you can make.

4. You Will Use Your Leverage Power

One of the main ideas behind wealth acceleration is leverage. To achieve exponential development, learn how to make the most of your time, money, and resources. Find ways to multiply your efforts and get better outcomes with less work, whether it's through using other people's resources (time, money, or experience), systems, technology, or strategic initiatives. In the Fastlane, embrace the power of leverage to multiply your wealth-building endeavours and establish enduring riches.

5. You Must Protect and Diversify Your Assets

Long-term performance and wealth preservation depend heavily on diversification and asset protection. Investing in a diverse range of businesses, asset classes, and geographical areas can help you spread risk and reduce your exposure to market volatility. Use risk management techniques to secure your assets and guard against unanticipated events, such as asset allocation, insurance, and estate preparation. Put capital preservation and risk reduction first to make sure your wealth is resilient and sustainable over time.

6. You Will Accept Failure and Take Reasonable Risks

Taking risks is a necessary component of wealth acceleration. Take measured chances and step outside your comfort zone to seize possibilities for personal development and accomplish your objectives. Recognise that failure is a necessary step on the path to success rather than a setback. Acknowledge your errors, adjust to new situations, and continue in the face of difficulty. Accept failure as a necessary component of the learning process and a chance for development and creativity in your quest to accumulate money.

7. You Must Develop an Attractive Mindset

Developing a wealth consciousness is a prerequisite to drawing abundance into your life. Adopt habits, attitudes, and beliefs that are consistent with wealth and success. Act as though success is already yours, visualise your objectives, and validate your dreams. As you embark on your wealth-building journey, surround yourself with uplifting people, role models that inspire you, and encouraging communities. Acquire an attitude of thankfulness, abundance, and giving, understanding that money comes to those

FASTLANE FORTUNE

who live according to the precepts of prosperity and plenty.

8. You Will Contribute and Change Things

True prosperity and success are characterised by giving back and changing the world. Make a significant difference on other people's lives and the globe by using your wealth and influence. Discover methods to support causes and organisations that share your beliefs and interests, whether it is through philanthropy, volunteer work, or social entrepreneurship. Keep in mind that the actual measure of wealth is not just the possessions you amass, but also the constructive contributions you make to society and the environment.

9. You Must Promote an Innovative and Adaptable Culture*

In a world that is changing quickly, innovation and adaptation are crucial for keeping ahead of the curve. Adopt an innovative culture that promotes experimentation, creativity, and forward-thinking ideas. Keep up with new developments in the market, disruptive technology, and emerging trends, and be prepared to modify your business plans and tactics as necessary. You may take advantage of new possibilities, overcome obstacles, and stay ahead of the curve in the Fastlane of wealth creation by cultivating a culture of

FASTLANE FORTUNE

innovation and adaptation.

10. You Must Develop Strategic Networks and Relationships

Networks and strategic partnerships are priceless tools for accelerating wealth. Develop connections with like-minded people, business titans, and powerful contacts who can help, advise, and stand up for you on your path to accumulating riches. Make the time and effort to create deep connections, go to networking gatherings, and join mastermind groups that offer chances for growth, learning, and cooperation. Building strategic alliances and networks can help you get more exposure, open doors, and move quickly towards success in the fast lane.

11. You Must Exercise Self-Control and Delay in Rewarding Behaviour

The keys to accelerating riches are self-control and postponing gratification. Develop the self-control to postpone instant enjoyment and make calculated short-term sacrifices in order to reap long-term benefits. Adopt responsible budgeting, saving, and money management practices that put long-term wealth building ahead of enjoyment. Gain the forbearance to endure through turbulence, stay the course, and withstand snap judgements that

FASTLANE FORTUNE

jeopardise your financial objectives. You can establish the groundwork for long-term success and wealth in the Fastlane by abstaining from instant gratification and exercising discipline.

12. You Must Always Innovate and Rework

The acceleration of wealth is mostly driven by ongoing invention and iteration. Adopt an attitude of innovation and continuous improvement, looking for new and innovative methods to better your processes, services, and goods. To find opportunities for innovation and development, get input from stakeholders, consumers, and market trends. Try out fresh concepts, strategies, and company plans to keep your wealth-building ventures growing and ahead of the competition. You can take advantage of new possibilities, adjust to shifting market dynamics, and succeed long-term and sustainably in the Fastlane by consistently inventing and iterating.

13. You Must Show Generosity and Gratitude

To draw prosperity and contentment into your life, you must cultivate an attitude of thankfulness and generosity. Develop an attitude of thankfulness for all the chances and benefits you have, and recognise the abundance all around you. Whether via journaling, meditation, or deeds of kindness, express appreciation on a regular basis and develop an outward-looking spirit of generosity. Give back to the community, lend a hand with resources, and support causes that align with your passions and values. You can experience more fulfilment and purpose in your wealth-building path as well as draw more riches into your life by cultivating appreciation and generosity.

14. You Must Continue to Be humble and open-minded

Being open-minded and humble are two qualities that will help you accelerate your wealth. In spite of your success, maintain your humility by appreciating the efforts of others and realising that you are a part of a wider ecosystem. Keep an open mind to fresh concepts, viewpoints, and opportunities while acknowledging that there is always more to learn and uncover. Develop a growth attitude that welcomes criticism as a way to keep getting better, welcomes challenges, and views failure as a teaching opportunity. You can handle the challenges of the Fastlane with grace, honesty, and resiliency if you maintain your humility and open-mindedness.

15. You Must Live a Life of Integrity and Purpose

The secret to real wealth and success is to live a life of integrity and purpose. Determine your life's values, interests, and purpose, then match your deeds to your greatest goals and ambitions. Knowing that your reputation and character are priceless assets in the process of accelerating your wealth, conduct yourself in all of your dealings with honesty, integrity, and transparency. Make choices that are consistent with your moral principles, further the common good, and provide a lasting legacy for future generations. Along the way of building money, leading a purposeful and honest life brings you fulfilment, relevance, and meaning in addition to financial success.

FASTLANE FORTUNE

Manage Time, Manage Wealth**

Comprehending the Connection Between Wealth and Time

Possibly the most important resource in the quest for prosperity is time. Time is a limited and irreplaceable resource, unlike money or other tangible belongings. Your capacity to generate and amass riches can be strongly impacted by the way you decide to use and distribute your time. Realising the connection between wealth and time is crucial to realising your full potential and reaching financial independence.

Putting High-Value Activities First

Setting high-value activities that support your wealth-building objectives as your top priorities is the first step in controlling time to control wealth. Decide which assignments and endeavours have the best chance of producing revenue, adding value, or advancing your financial goals. provide your time and attention to projects that will provide you the best return on investment (ROI); assign or do away with any operations that will consume your resources but won't improve your bottom line. Setting high-value tasks as your top priorities can help you make the most of your time and reach your full wealth-building potential.

Developing Effective Time Management Skills

Being able to manage your time well is essential to controlling your wealth. To maximise productivity and efficiency, master time management strategies including goal setting, prioritising, and scheduling. Establish definite, well-defined objectives for your wealth-building pursuits and divide them into manageable assignments with due dates. Sort jobs into priority lists according to their significance and urgency, making sure to concentrate on high-impact projects that support your goals. To help you remain on track with your financial objectives and streamline your workflow, try using time-tracking apps, calendars, and to-do lists.

Delegating and Automating Regular Tasks

Delegation and automation are effective time management techniques that free up resources for wealth-building endeavours. Determine which low-value or routine jobs can be assigned to others or automated with technology. Use software and technologies to automate time-consuming tasks like bookkeeping, customer service, and email marketing. To free up time for higher-level strategic work, assign duties to virtual assistants, freelancers, or trusted team members. You may increase your productivity and efficiency and free up more time for wealth development by automating and assigning regular activities.

Investing in Development and Personal Growth

Putting money into one's own personal development is another strategy for managing time and riches. Seek for possibilities for self-improvement, skill development, and learning all the time so that you can grow your abilities and become more valuable to employers. Participate in training programmes, workshops, and seminars to broaden your knowledge, pick up new skills, and keep up with business trends. Invest in mastermind groups, coaching, or mentoring to receive direction, accountability, and support on your wealth-building path. You may build a more successful and happy life and hasten your path to financial success by making investments in your own personal growth and development.

Preserving Your Energy and Time

Maintaining concentration and momentum in your wealth-building endeavours requires that you protect your time and energy. To prevent distractions and time-wasting activities, set boundaries and prioritise tasks. Saying no to chances and commitments that conflict with your principles or aims is a valuable skill. You should also learn to assign or outsource work that consumes your time or diverts your attention. Maintaining your physical and mental health via self-care and stress management will give you the stamina and fortitude to go after your wealth-building objectives head-on.

Building Processes and Systems for Efficiency

In order to maximise efficiency and scalability in your wealth-building endeavours, you must create systems and processes. Create standardised norms, procedures, and workflows to reduce friction in your operations and expedite repetitive jobs. Automate repetitive tasks with technology, like as inventory management, invoicing, and customer onboarding, to cut down on manual involvement and free up time for more high-level strategic endeavours. To make sure you are maximising your efficiency and effectiveness in your quest of money, keep an eye on and enhance your systems and processes on a constant basis.

Solve Needs, Reap Rewards**

Understanding the Principle of Solving Needs

At its core, entrepreneurship and wealth creation revolve around solving needs. The principle is simple: identify a problem or need that exists in the market, develop a solution to address it, and deliver value to those who need it most. By solving needs effectively, entrepreneurs can create products, services, and businesses that not only meet the demands of consumers but also generate substantial rewards and financial returns.

Identifying Market Needs and Pain Points

The first step in solving needs to reap rewards is identifying market needs and pain points. Conduct thorough market research to identify gaps, inefficiencies, or problems that exist in the marketplace. Listen to the feedback of customers, analyze industry trends, and study competitor offerings to gain insights into areas where you can add value and differentiate yourself from the competition. By identifying market needs and pain points,

FASTLANE FORTUNE

entrepreneurs can uncover lucrative opportunities for innovation and disruption.

Developing Innovative Solutions

Once market needs and pain points have been identified, the next step is to develop innovative solutions to address them. This may involve brainstorming ideas, prototyping concepts, and testing hypotheses to determine the viability and feasibility of potential solutions. Embrace creativity, experimentation, and iteration as you develop and refine your offerings, seeking feedback from customers and stakeholders to ensure that your solutions effectively meet their needs and expectations. By developing innovative solutions that solve real-world problems, entrepreneurs can create products and services that resonate with consumers and drive demand in the marketplace.

Delivering Value and Creating Impact

FASTLANE FORTUNE

The ultimate goal of solving needs is to deliver value and create impact for customers, stakeholders, and society at large. Focus on creating solutions that provide tangible benefits, solve problems, and improve the lives of those you serve. Whether it's improving efficiency, enhancing convenience, or enhancing quality of life, prioritize delivering value that exceeds customer expectations and generates positive outcomes. By creating value and making a meaningful impact, entrepreneurs can build trust, loyalty, and goodwill with their target audience, laying the foundation for long-term success and sustainable growth.

Monetizing Solutions and Capturing Value

In addition to delivering value, entrepreneurs must also monetize their solutions effectively to reap rewards and generate sustainable revenue streams. Explore different monetization strategies, such as direct sales, subscriptions, licensing, or advertising, to determine the most appropriate pricing model for your offerings. Consider the perceived value of your solutions, competitive pricing benchmarks, and customer willingness to pay as you establish pricing tiers and revenue streams. By capturing value and monetizing your solutions effectively, entrepreneurs can generate revenue, recoup investments, and achieve profitability in their wealth-building endeavors.

Scaling Impact and Expanding Reach

As your solutions gain traction and momentum in the marketplace, focus on scaling impact and expanding reach to maximize your rewards and amplify your influence. Explore opportunities for growth, such as entering new markets, expanding product lines, or forming strategic partnerships, to reach a broader audience and penetrate new segments. Leverage technology, automation, and systems to streamline operations, optimize efficiency, and scale your business operations effectively. By scaling impact and expanding reach, entrepreneurs can magnify their rewards and achieve greater success in the Fastlane of wealth creation.

Building Sustainable Businesses and Long-Term Value

Finally, focus on building sustainable businesses that create long-term value for all stakeholders involved. Prioritize ethical business practices, social responsibility, and environmental sustainability as you grow and expand your operations. Cultivate a culture of innovation, integrity, and excellence within your organization, fostering collaboration, creativity, and continuous improvement. By building sustainable businesses that prioritize people, planet, and profit, entrepreneurs can create lasting value, generate enduring rewards, and leave a positive legacy for future generations.

Growth Is Required: Scale or Fail

FASTLANE FORTUNE

Aware of the Importance of Scaling

The tenet of "scale or fail" emphasises the necessity of growth and expansion for long-term success and sustainability in the ever-changing world of business and entrepreneurship. The process of growing a company's size, breadth, or reach in order to take advantage of opportunities, increase productivity, and make a bigger impression on customers is known as scaling. Scaling is crucial for sustaining competitiveness, spurring innovation, and gaining traction in the modern global economy, whether it is through broadening market reach, varying product offers, or boosting operational capacity.

The Dangers of Stability

Stasis is the same as failure in a corporate environment that is changing quickly. Inability to grow and adjust to shifting consumer demands, market conditions, and technology developments can result in irrelevance, obsolescence, and eventually company failure. Businesses that don't adapt and expand run the risk of falling behind their competitors who innovate and upend established industries, forcing them to watch from the sidelines as others take advantage of openings and gain market share. Businesses face stagnation, decline, and the imminent prospect of extinction when they do not grow and expand.

Opening Doors for Growth

There are numerous options for organisations to harness growth potential and reach higher success levels through scaling. Through market expansion, income stream diversification, and innovation investment, organisations can leverage unexplored prospects and establish themselves for sustained success. By scaling, companies can take advantage of economies of scale, improve operational effectiveness, and reduce expenses, which leads to increased profitability and long-term growth. Additionally, scaling enables companies to draw in top personnel, establish strategic alliances, and get access to the financing resources required to support growth and innovation.

* Fulfilling Client Requests*

In today's fiercely competitive industry, scaling is necessary to satisfy customers' changing needs and expectations. Businesses need to change and adapt as consumer tastes do in order to provide experiences, goods, and services that appeal to their target market. By scaling, companies may react instantly to the shifting demands, tastes, and market trends of their clientele, maintaining their competitiveness and relevance in their eyes. Businesses may increase consumer satisfaction, foster brand loyalty, and forge a strong market presence that propels long-term success and profitability by growing effectively.

Achieving Excellence in Operations

Operational excellence and scaling go hand in hand, allowing companies to maximise performance, productivity, and efficiency in all aspect of their operations. Businesses can increase productivity and save expenses by streamlining workflows, removing bottlenecks, and optimising resource allocation through the implementation of scalable systems, processes, and technologies. Businesses that scale are also better able to draw in and hold on to top personnel, promote innovation, and create a dynamic work atmosphere that encourages teamwork and creativity. Businesses can put themselves in the Fastlane of business for long-term success and sustainable growth by establishing operational excellence.

Welcoming Adaptation and Innovation

Businesses must embrace innovation and adaptation as

fundamental components of their growth strategy in order to scale. Agility and flexibility are critical in today's fast-paced business world because they allow organisations to react swiftly to shifting market conditions, new trends, and disruptive technology. Through cultivating an environment that values creativity, trial and error, and ongoing enhancement, companies can maintain a competitive edge, grasp novel prospects, and set themselves apart from rivals. In addition, scaling necessitates that companies modify their organisational structures, business plans, and strategies to allow for growth and expansion while maintaining their flexibility and resilience in the face of change and uncertainty.

The Benefits of Growing

Even if scaling has its share of difficulties and complications, the benefits are well worth the work. Companies can establish themselves as leaders in their sector and increase shareholder value by scaling successfully and achieving higher levels of profitability, market share, and brand recognition. Businesses can also benefit from scaling by generating employment, promoting economic expansion, and improving the communities they operate in. Furthermore, scaling enables business owners to achieve their goals, follow their interests, and leave a lasting legacy that goes well beyond their financial success.

CHAPTER 5

FASTLANE STRATEGIES

Working cleverly is more important for success in the Fastlane of wealth development and entrepreneurship than working hard. By utilising creative thinking, grasping chances, and optimising productivity, fastlane tactics are intended to assist people and companies in quickening their path to financial success. Entrepreneurs can accelerate their journey to financial independence and establish enduring wealth in the ever-changing business environment of today by adopting these tactics.

1. Adopt a Growth Mentality

The first step to success in the Fastlane is embracing a growth mindset, which is the conviction that talent, intelligence, and talents can be acquired via commitment, hard work, and persistence. See obstacles as chances for improvement, see failures as teaching moments, and remain optimistic in the face of difficulty. Develop an optimistic, resilient, and abundant mindset that will enable you to take advantage of chances, get past setbacks, and accomplish your goals in the Fastlane.

FASTLANE FORTUNE

2. Have Big Ideas, Start Small

To achieve amazing achievements in the Fastlane, big thinking is necessary. Aspirational goals should be set, bold ambitions should be had, and an endless future should be imagined. But as vital as it is to imagine big, it is just as necessary to start small. Your progress will be made step by step if you break down your goals into doable, achievable measures. You may achieve your goals and fulfil your vision of success in the Fastlane by starting small and generating momentum over time.

3. Pay Attention to High-Impact Tasks

Time is a valuable resource that needs to be used carefully in the Fastlane. Put all of your time and effort into high-impact projects that will make a difference in your wealth-building efforts. Give top priority to the jobs and initiatives that have the most potential to improve your goals, produce revenue, or add value. Assign or remove low-value tasks that don't improve your bottom line, and set strict time priorities to make sure your attention is being directed towards projects that will yield the highest return on investment (ROI).

4. Utilise Automation and Technology

FASTLANE FORTUNE

Technology can help entrepreneurs succeed in the Fastlane by giving them the tools and resources they need to maximise productivity, streamline processes, and grow their companies quickly. Use technology and automation to remove time-consuming manual processes that waste resources and automate repetitive operations and workflows. To work smarter, not harder, invest in productivity tools, digital platforms, and software solutions. Then, concentrate your attention on high-value tasks that propel innovation and success in your company.

5. Establish Robust Connections and Networks

In order to succeed in the Fastlane, one must work as a team and collaborate with others as well as network with peers in the field. Cultivate robust connections and alliances with fellow entrepreneurs, mentors, advisors, and influential individuals who may offer direction, encouragement, and prospects for advancement. To increase your impact and make connections with people who can assist you in achieving your objectives in the Fastlane, go to networking events, enrol in mastermind groups, and take part in industry associations.

6. Adjust and Create

FASTLANE FORTUNE

Being flexible and innovative is crucial in the Fastlane to be one step ahead of the competition and take advantage of new possibilities and trends. In reaction to evolving consumer tastes, market dynamics, and technology breakthroughs, be prepared to modify your company model, adjust your strategy, and welcome change. To set yourself apart from competition and develop a special value proposition that appeals to your target market, innovate constantly, try out novel concepts, and venture into unexplored territory.

7. Make Education and Personal Growth Investments

Success in the Fastlane requires constant learning and self-improvement since it helps business owners gain new abilities, increase their knowledge base, and outperform rivals. Make an investment in your education by going to conferences, seminars, and workshops as well as taking online courses that offer knowledge and insights pertinent to your field and objectives. Look for advisors, coaches, and mentors who can provide direction, responsibility, and support while you negotiate the opportunities and challenges of the Fastlane. You may hone your abilities, extend your perspective, and put yourself in a successful position in the cutthroat corporate world of today by making an investment in your education and personal growth.

8. Take Reasonable Chances

Taking risks is an essential component of the Fastlane path to success. Seeking your goals and ambitions requires you to be open to embracing uncertainty, taking calculated chances, and stepping beyond of your comfort zone. Make educated decisions based on facts, analysis, and intuition by carefully evaluating the risks involved and balancing the possible benefits against the possible drawbacks. See failure as an opportunity for learning, development, and resilience in the Fastlane and accept that it is not a setback but rather a necessary step on the path to success.

9. Foster Perseverance and Resilience

In the Fastlane, tenacity and resilience are essential traits for success. Anticipate difficulties, problems, and roadblocks along the route, but keep your resolve to keep going when things become tough. Resilience can be developed by seeing obstacles as transitory rather than insurmountable, and by taking lessons from each failure to become stronger, smarter, and more driven to achieve. Accept failure as a necessary component of the learning process and use it to strengthen your will to keep going until you reach your objectives in the Fastlane.

10. Make health and wellbeing a priority

Achieving success in the Fastlane demands not only business acumen but also physical and emotional health. Make your health and well-being a priority by forming wholesome routines that include consistent exercise, a balanced diet, enough sleep, and stress reduction methods. Allocate time for restorative pursuits that revitalise your mind, body, and soul, like yoga, meditation, or enjoyable hobbies. To guarantee that you have the stamina, determination, and energy necessary to excel in the Fastlane, keep in mind that your health is your most precious asset and give it top priority.

11. Promote an Innovative and Creative Culture

Creativity and innovation are essential for success in the Fastlane. Encourage your team members to think creatively, explore, and be curious in order to cultivate an innovative culture within your company. Establish a space where concepts are accepted, investigated, and tested without concern for approval or disapproval. Give your staff the freedom to think creatively, question the established quo, and go after audacious concepts that could upend whole sectors and spur expansion. You may open up new doors, find solutions to challenging issues, and stay one step ahead of the competitors in the Fastlane by cultivating a culture of innovation and creativity.

12. Exercise Prudence and Financial Discipline

To succeed in the Fastlane, you must have sound financial judgement and discipline, which will help you allocate your resources sensibly and make choices that will help you achieve your long-term objectives. Be economical and cut out pointless spending, allocating your funds to endeavours that will yield the best return on investment (ROI) and propel your company's expansion. Make sure you are living within your means and avoiding excessive debt or financial risk by creating a budget, keeping track of your spending, and routinely monitoring your cash flow. You can improve your financial situation, reduce risk, and lay the groundwork for long-term success and happiness in the Fastlane by exercising financial restraint and discipline.

13. Encourage an Ownership and Accountability Culture

In order to succeed in the Fastlane and generate outcomes, accountability and ownership are crucial. Create a culture of accountability in your company by outlining each team member's position, responsibility, and expectations. Promote candid feedback, open communication, and openness while holding people responsible for their deeds and results. Give your staff the freedom to own their work, ideas, and projects so they may feel proud, accountable, and responsible for everything they do. It is possible to build a high-performing team that is dedicated to attaining excellence and accelerating results in the Fastlane by cultivating an environment of accountability and ownership.

14. Request Input for Ongoing Improvement

Success in the Fastlane is characterised by continuous improvement, which helps you to change, develop, and expand in response to shifting consumer demands and market conditions. Regularly solicit input from stakeholders, consumers, and staff to find areas where your goods, services, and business practices may use some innovation and improvement. Accept constructive criticism as a chance for development and learning, and make use of it to improve your methods, procedures, and products. Adhere to an improvement-oriented culture in which every achievement and setback is seen as a chance to grow, learn, and change as you pursue excellence in the Fastlane.

15. Repay and Give It Away

In the Fastlane, success entails more than just maximising one's own profits; it also entails improving the lives of others and giving back to the community. Adopt a generous and philanthropic mindset by lending your support to projects, groups, and causes that share your interests and values. Find ways to give back and pay it forward in the Fastlane, whether it's by volunteering in your neighbourhood, lending a hand to aspiring business owners, or donating time, money, or resources to charitable organisations. You may make a lasting positive impression on the world and establish an impactful legacy by improving the lives of others.

CHAPTER 6

Fueling Your Fastlane Journey: Strategies for Sustainable Growth

In the Fastlane of entrepreneurship and wealth creation, success is fueled by a combination of ambition, innovation, and strategic execution. However, sustaining momentum and achieving long-term success requires a well-defined strategy for fueling your Fastlane journey. From cultivating resilience and adaptability to nurturing relationships and embracing innovation, there are several key strategies that can help entrepreneurs navigate the challenges and opportunities of the Fastlane while staying on course toward their goals.

1. Cultivate Resilience and Adaptability

Resilience and adaptability are essential qualities for navigating the twists and turns of the Fastlane journey. Embrace challenges as opportunities for growth, and view setbacks as valuable learning experiences rather than insurmountable obstacles. Cultivate resilience by maintaining a positive mindset, staying flexible in the face of change, and seeking support from mentors, peers, and advisors during challenging times. By cultivating resilience and adaptability, you can weather the inevitable ups and downs of entrepreneurship and emerge stronger, wiser, and more prepared to tackle whatever comes your way in the Fastlane.

2. Foster Strategic Partnerships and Alliances

Strategic partnerships and alliances can provide valuable resources, expertise, and opportunities for growth in the Fastlane. Collaborate with complementary businesses, industry leaders, and strategic partners who share your vision and values, and explore opportunities for mutual benefit and collaboration. By fostering strategic partnerships and alliances, you can access new markets, expand your reach, and leverage complementary strengths and resources to accelerate your growth and achieve your goals more efficiently and effectively.

3. Invest in Continuous Learning and Development

Continuous learning and development are essential for staying ahead of the curve and fueling your Fastlane journey with fresh ideas, insights, and skills. Invest in your own education and professional development by attending seminars, workshops, and conferences, and enrolling in online courses or certification programs relevant to your industry and goals. Seek out mentors, coaches, and advisors who can offer guidance, support, and accountability as you navigate the challenges and opportunities of the Fastlane. By investing in continuous learning and development, you can stay at the forefront of innovation, adapt to changing market conditions, and position yourself for long-term success and prosperity in the Fastlane.

4. Embrace Innovation and Creativity

Innovation and creativity are the lifeblood of success in the Fastlane, enabling entrepreneurs to differentiate themselves, solve complex problems, and create value in new and innovative ways. Embrace a culture of innovation and creativity within your organization by encouraging experimentation, exploration, and out-of-the-box thinking among your team members. Foster an environment where ideas are welcomed, tested, and refined, and empower your employees to take risks and pursue bold ideas that have the potential to disrupt industries and drive growth. By embracing innovation and creativity, you can unlock new opportunities, solve complex problems, and stay ahead of the competition in the Fastlane.

5. Prioritize Customer Satisfaction and Retention

Customer satisfaction and retention are paramount in the Fastlane, as loyal customers are the lifeblood of any successful business. Prioritize customer satisfaction by delivering exceptional products, services, and experiences that exceed customer expectations and create lasting value. Invest in customer relationship management (CRM) systems and tools to track customer interactions, gather feedback, and personalize your offerings to meet individual customer needs and preferences. By prioritizing customer satisfaction and retention, you can build a loyal customer base, drive repeat business, and generate positive word-of-mouth referrals that fuel your Fastlane journey with sustainable growth and success.

6. Leverage Technology and Automation

Technology and automation are powerful tools for fueling your Fastlane journey with efficiency, scalability, and productivity. Invest in cutting-edge technologies, software solutions, and digital platforms that streamline your operations, optimize your workflows, and automate repetitive tasks and processes. Leverage artificial intelligence (AI), machine learning, and data analytics to gain insights into customer behavior, market trends, and business performance, enabling you to make informed decisions and drive growth more effectively. By leveraging technology and automation, you can free up time and resources to focus on high-value activities that drive innovation, growth, and success in the Fastlane.

7. Cultivate a Strong Company Culture

A strong company culture is the foundation of success in the Fastlane, fostering loyalty, engagement, and alignment among your team members and stakeholders. Cultivate a culture of transparency, integrity, and accountability that empowers your employees to take ownership of their work, collaborate effectively, and contribute to the success of the organization. Recognize and reward employees who embody your company values and make meaningful contributions to your mission and goals, and create

FASTLANE FORTUNE

opportunities for professional growth, development, and advancement within your organization. By cultivating a strong company culture, you can attract top talent, retain key employees, and create a dynamic, high-performing team that drives growth and success in the Fastlane.

Developing Routines for Optimal Output and Efficiency**

High performance and productivity are critical characteristics that set the exceptional apart from the ordinary in the pursuit of success. Establishing routines that promote efficiency and optimal performance is essential to reaching your objectives and reaching your maximum potential. Creating habits that increase your productivity can have a big impact on your performance in both your personal and professional lives, whether you're a student, professional, or entrepreneur.

1. Create a Morning Schedule

Your morning ritual can have a big impact on your productivity and mentality, as well as setting the tone for the remainder of the day. Create a morning routine that includes exercises, journaling, meditation, or goal-setting to help you start your day with intention. Starting your day with mentally, physically, and spiritually nourishing activities can help you feel more energised, improve your focus, and position yourself for maximum productivity and excellent performance.

FASTLANE FORTUNE

2. Set Clear Goals and Prioritise Tasks

Time management skills are essential for good performance and productivity. Sort jobs according to their urgency and importance, and make sure your daily actions are guided by specific, attainable goals. Divide more ambitious aims into more manageable activities, and rank them according to how they will affect your main goals. You can increase your productivity and accomplish more in less time by concentrating your time and effort on activities that are in line with your targets and priorities.

3. Employ the Pomodoro Technique and Time Blocking

Two effective time management and productivity boosters are time blocking and the Pomodoro Technique. By setting aside certain blocks of time for various jobs or activities, time blocking enables you to concentrate on one task at a time without interruptions. Using the Pomodoro Technique, you should divide your work into manageable chunks of time—typically 25 minutes—and take a brief rest in between. You can sustain high levels of productivity and focus throughout the day by alternating between moments of concentrated work and rest.

4. Reduce Interruptions and Distractions

Your concentration and productivity might be disrupted by interruptions and distractions, which makes it difficult to achieve your objectives. By turning off notifications, muting your phone, and setting up a separate workplace free from distractions, you may reduce distractions in advance. Establish boundaries with friends, family, and coworkers to reduce disruptions during moments of concentrated work. You should also set aside specific times for monitoring social media, email, and other non-essential duties. You can stay focused and productive and get more done in less time by reducing interruptions and distractions.

5. Engage in Stress Reduction and Mindfulness

You may maintain your composure, resilience, and focus in the midst of difficulties and pressure by practicing mindfulness and stress management practices. To lower stress, raise self-awareness, and improve focus, incorporate mindfulness exercises like yoga, meditation, or deep breathing into your everyday routine. Make self-care activities that support general balance and well-being a priority, and take regular pauses throughout the day to refresh and rejuvenate your body and mind. Over time, you can develop a positive outlook, boost your resilience, and maintain high performance and productivity levels by engaging in mindfulness and stress management practices.

6. Always Learn and Get Better

In today's fast-paced environment, staying ahead requires constant learning and self-improvement. Set aside time every day to pursue chances for professional and personal development, learn new skills, and gain knowledge. Discover mentors, coaches, or advisers who can provide direction and support along the journey. You can also read books, listen to podcasts, attend workshops, or sign up for courses that match your interests and ambitions. You may increase your skills, remain current in your industry, and seize fresh chances for development and success by never stopping learning and getting better.

7. Adopt a Growth Mentality

A growth mindset is necessary to reach optimal productivity and performance levels. Accept obstacles as chances for personal development, and see failures as priceless lessons rather than as setbacks. Have faith in your capacity to grow and change over time, and embrace learning, trying new things, and personal development. You may overcome challenges, go beyond your comfort zone, and experience more success and fulfilment in both your personal and professional life by adopting a growth mindset.

Investing in Your Development: Networks, Education, and Skills

One of the best things you can do for yourself is to invest in your own development. You can improve your abilities, progress your career, and find more success and fulfilment in both your personal and professional life by consistently learning new things, acquiring new skills, and cultivating professional relationships. Let's discuss the value of utilising networks, education, and skill development to invest in your personal development.

1. Education: Increasing Your Understanding

The basis for both professional and personal development is education, which gives you the skills and understanding required to deal with the challenges of today's complicated world. You can deepen your understanding of a variety of subjects, learn new skills, and stay up to date with industry trends and developments by investing in education, whether through formal education—attending college or university—or informal learning opportunities—online courses, workshops, or self-study. You may improve your ability to solve problems, make wise decisions, and seize new possibilities for personal and professional growth and progress by consistently broadening your knowledge base.

2. Developing Your Skills: Increasing Your Capabilities

Maintaining competitiveness in today's quickly changing labour market and economy requires investing in skill development. You may set yourself apart from competitors, become more valuable as an employee or business owner, and keep up with technological changes and shifting market demands by making an investment in the development of new skills. Whether it's developing specialised expertise in a particular field, refining soft skills like leadership, communication, or critical thinking, or learning technical skills pertinent to your line of work, investing in skills development allows you to grow professionally, increase career opportunities, and succeed and feel more fulfilled in your chosen field.

3. Networks: Developing Business Connections

Building a network through networking can help you grow personally and professionally by giving you access to opportunities, resources, and support systems that will help you succeed more quickly. You can increase the size of your professional network, obtain viewpoints and insights from a variety of thought leaders and industry experts, and open up new career, mentoring, and collaborative opportunities by making an investment in developing and maintaining professional relationships. Participating in online communities and forums, attending industry events, or joining professional organisations are all examples of how investing in your networks can help you to forge deep connections, develop your personal brand, and gain access to a multitude of resources that can help you reach new heights in terms of success and growth

Sustainable Speed in the Balance: Long-Term Wealth vs Short-Term Gains

There is frequently conflict between the need for long-term sustainability and the need for rapid profits in the chase of wealth development and financial success. Even while getting results quickly can be alluring, it's important to weigh the benefits and drawbacks of choosing short-term earnings over long-term wealth building. In order to achieve long-term prosperity and financial stability, balancing speed with sustainability necessitates giving your financial goals, risk tolerance, and investing strategy significant thought.

1. Quick Profits: The Allure of Instantaneous Outcomes

FASTLANE FORTUNE

The term "short-term gains" describes the rapid returns or profits that come from day trading, speculative investing, and other high-risk, high-reward techniques. The attraction of short-term gains is their capacity to generate wealth quickly and provide instant satisfaction, luring investors in with the prospect of big returns and overnight success. Though they can provide instant benefits, short-term profits are frequently associated with higher levels of risk and volatility. This makes them vulnerable to changes in the market and unanticipated events, which can quickly deplete wealth.

2. The Advantages of Patience and Persistence for Long-Term Wealth

Conversely, long-term wealth is constructed on a foundation of discipline, patience, and strategic planning. Long-term wealth accumulation prioritises compounding returns over time and sustainable growth over short-term benefits. Investing in assets with solid growth potential and solid fundamentals helps investors weather short-term market swings and increase the stability and durability of their investment portfolios. The benefits of long-term wealth, such as financial security, passive income, and generational wealth, make the journey time- and patience-consuming, but it is well worth it.

*3. The Need for Balance: Sustainability vs. Speed.

Achieving long-term prosperity and financial security requires striking a balance between speed and sustainability. Even though certain market circumstances or investing techniques may present opportunities for short-term advantages, it's critical to assess the risks and benefits and think about the long-term effects of your decisions. Long-term financial instability and failures might result from rushing into speculative investments or chasing fast rewards without taking the underlying fundamentals and hazards into consideration. Instead, give priority to techniques that support long-term wealth accumulation and sustainable growth, and concentrate on assembling a diverse portfolio of assets that are in line with your financial objectives, risk tolerance, and time horizon.

4. Techniques for Juggling Sustainability and Speed

Investors have various options at their disposal to attain long-term wealth building while striking a balance between speed and sustainability.

- Diversification: To lower risk and improve portfolio resilience, distribute your investments over a variety of asset classes, industries, and geographical areas.
- Dollar-cost averaging: To mitigate market volatility and seize long-term growth opportunities, invest consistently over an extended period of time, irrespective of market conditions.
- Put an emphasis on fundamentals: To reduce risk and increase long-term returns, give top priority to investments in assets with good fundamentals, such as consistent earnings growth, steady cash flow, and competitive advantages.
- Avoid following trends: Instead of focusing on investments with a track record of success and room to develop, resist the urge to follow fads or speculative ventures without a strong base.
- Retain a long-term perspective: Remain committed to your long-term financial objectives and fight the impulse to act rashly in response to transient market movements or noise.

FASTLANE FORTUNE

CHAPTER 7

Moving Through the Fast Lane: Effective Success Techniques

The fast-paced pursuit of achievement, financial independence, and personal fulfilment are hallmarks of the Fastlane lifestyle. In today's fast-paced and dynamic world, navigating this lifestyle calls for a blend of resilience, adaptability, and strategic thinking. Whether you're an aspirational professional, investor, or entrepreneur, figuring out how to live in the Fastlane is crucial to reaching your objectives and building a prosperous and abundant life.

1. Establish Your Priorities and Goals

Establishing your objectives and goals precisely is the first step towards living the Fastlane lifestyle. Set challenging but attainable goals that are consistent with your values and aspirations after taking some time to consider what matters most to you in life, both personally and professionally. Whether your objectives are to create a profitable company, become financially independent, or improve the world, living the Fastlane lifestyle will be easier for you to navigate if you have a clear sense of purpose and direction.

2. Develop a Growth Mentality

Success in the Fastlane requires a growth mindset because it allows you to rise to difficulties, learn from setbacks, and develop personally and professionally over time. Develop an optimistic, resilient, and inquisitive mindset that enables you to see failures as teaching moments, challenges as chances for personal development, and achievement as a process rather than a goal. You may overcome hardship, go beyond your comfort zone, and experience more success and fulfilment in the Fastlane lifestyle by embracing a growth mindset.

3. Accept Uncertainty and Risk

In order to pursue your goals and objectives, you must be willing to venture outside of your comfort zone, embrace danger, and live in the fast lane. Recognise that taking calculated risks is a necessary component of being an entrepreneur and that failing is a necessary step towards success rather than a setback. Accept uncertainty as a chance for development and creativity, and be prepared to change course as necessary to meet unforeseen obstacles and shifting market conditions. You can seize fresh possibilities, push the envelope of what's feasible, and accomplish remarkable feats in the Fastlane lifestyle by accepting risk and uncertainty.

4. Give work-life balance top priority

Despite the ambition and energy that define the Fastlane lifestyle, work-life balance must be given top priority in order to prevent burnout and preserve general wellbeing. Establish boundaries between your personal and professional lives, and schedule time for pursuits like hobbies, exercise, and quality time with loved ones that are good for your mind, body, and soul. Recall that success involves more than just reaching your financial objectives; it also entails leading a happy, purposeful life that incorporates all facets of your existence. You can maintain your energy and attention over time and relish the experience of navigating the Fastlane lifestyle by placing a high priority on work-life balance.

*5. Make an investment in your own personal development

To successfully navigate the Fastlane lifestyle, one must continually grow and develop personally. Invest in yourself by looking for chances to learn, grow, and acquire new skills that will broaden your horizons and improve your abilities. Make time for activities that will help you enhance your personal development and become the best version of yourself. These activities can include reading books, going to seminars, enrolling in courses, or contacting mentors and coaches. You may seize fresh chances, overcome obstacles, and experience more success and fulfilment in the Fastlane lifestyle by making an investment in your own personal growth and development.

6. Create a Network of Support

Establishing a robust support system is crucial for effectively managing the obstacles and prospects presented by the Fastlane way of life. As you pursue your goals and objectives, surround yourself with like-minded people, mentors, advisors, and peers who can provide direction, support, and encouragement. Join mastermind groups, look for networking opportunities, and build relationships with like-minded individuals who share your goals and values. You can obtain fresh possibilities, acquire insightful knowledge, and more skillfully negotiate the intricacies of the Fastlane lifestyle by establishing a support network.

7. Exercise Mindfulness and Gratitude

Maintaining perspective and being grounded in the middle of the fast-paced Fastlane lifestyle requires engaging in gratitude and mindfulness practices. Every day, set aside some time to count your blessings, give thanks for the experiences and opportunities you've had, and develop an appreciation for the here and now. Engage in mindfulness exercises like journaling, deep breathing, or meditation as part of your daily routine to develop resilience and inner calm in the midst of difficulties and uncertainty. As you negotiate the Fastlane lifestyle, you may create a positive mentality, lower stress levels, and improve your general well-being by engaging in mindfulness and appreciation practices.

Methods for Balancing Speed and Sustainability

Businesses and individuals in today's fast-paced environment frequently struggle to balance the demands of sustainability with the urgency of speed. While getting results quickly is ideal, we should also think about the long-term effects of our decisions and work towards success and growth that is sustainable. A strategic strategy that weighs short- and long-term goals and takes into account the social, environmental, and economic effects of our decisions is needed to strike a balance between sustainability and speed.

FASTLANE FORTUNE

1. Establish Priorities and Goals Clearly

Establishing priorities and goals that are consistent with your values and aspirations is the first step in striking a balance between sustainability and speed. Prioritise your short- and long-term goals according to their significance and influence on your overarching mission and vision. Clearly define your short-term and long-term objectives. You may concentrate your time, efforts, and resources on tasks that advance and add value while reducing interruptions and inefficiencies that undermine your sustainability efforts by setting clear objectives and priorities.

2. Implement Lean and Agile Methodologies

Agile and lean methodologies are useful instruments in today's fast-paced corporate world for striking a balance between sustainability and speed. By implementing agile approaches, you can quickly adapt to shifting client demands and market conditions, iterate on ideas and solutions fast, and provide stakeholders with value on time. In a similar vein, lean principles assist you in maximising efficiency and effectiveness by streamlining procedures, getting rid of waste, and optimising resource usage. You may increase the rate of innovation and growth while lowering the risk of burnout and resource depletion by implementing agile and lean principles.

3. Welcome Innovation and Ongoing Enhancement

Drive sustainability and speed at the same time requires innovation and constant improvement. Encourage your team members to think outside the box, be creative, and experiment to create an innovative culture within your company. Employees should be empowered to spot inefficiencies, make suggestions for improvements, and carry out actions that advance development and improve sustainability. You can stay ahead of the competition, adjust to shifting market conditions, and ultimately achieve sustainable growth and success by embracing innovation and continual improvement.

4. Strike a Balance Between Short-Term and Long-Term Goals

Effectively balancing sustainability and speed requires striking a balance between short- and long-term goals. While achieving fast victories and producing results is crucial, it's also critical to think about how your actions and decisions will affect the bigger picture in the long run. Consider the possible effects your projects may have on society, the environment, and the economy. Make an effort to match your short- and long-term objectives with your vision and core principles. Without sacrificing your commitment to sustainability, you can achieve sustainable growth and success by finding a balance between short- and long-term goals.

5. Encourage cooperation and alliances

In today's linked world, partnerships and collaboration are essential for sustainability and speed. Create strategic partnerships with stakeholders, industry partners, and organisations who share your commitment to sustainability so that you may work together to accomplish common objectives and move forward more quickly. Together, you may achieve greater sustainability and success by accelerating innovation, maximising your impact, and utilising each other's skills and experience through knowledge sharing and resource pooling.

6. Track and Evaluate Development

Efficient measurement and tracking are crucial for effectively managing sustainability and speed. To monitor your progress towards short- and long-term goals, set up metrics and key performance indicators (KPIs). Then, periodically assess and evaluate your results to pinpoint areas that could use optimisation. To stay on course and achieve long-term, sustainable growth and success, use data-driven insights to guide your decision-making process and make necessary adjustments to your strategy and tactics.

7. Develop Adaptability and Resilience

In today's environment of rapid change, resilience and adaptability are essential traits for balancing sustainability and speed. Anticipate difficulties, problems, and roadblocks along the route, and develop the fortitude to get through them with poise and resolve. Embrace failure as a normal part of the learning process and be prepared to pivot and adapt in reaction to unforeseen occurrences, developing trends, and shifting market conditions. You may traverse the challenges of sustainability and speed with confidence and resilience by developing resilience and adaptability, which will ultimately lead to greater success and fulfilment.

FASTLANE FORTUNE

Wealth Management: From Income Creation to Asset Defence

A comprehensive approach that includes a range of tactics and procedures to maximise financial resources, produce income, and safeguard assets throughout time is necessary for effective wealth management. Careful preparation, sound judgement, and an emphasis on long-term sustainability and security are necessary for managing wealth, from optimising earning potential to reducing risks and safeguarding wealth for future generations.

1. Creating Revenue: Optimising Earning Capabilities

Making the most of your earning potential in order to create revenue and establish a strong financial base is the first step in managing wealth. This entails making educational investments, learning useful skills, and seeking employment possibilities that line up with your interests, strengths, and financial objectives. Focus on producing several streams of income, whether via work, entrepreneurship, or investing activities, to diversify your sources of income and build stability and resilience in your financial portfolio.

2. Financial Planning and Budgeting

Effective wealth management requires both budgeting and financial planning since they enable you to set spending priorities, manage your money sensibly, and reach your financial objectives. To ensure financial discipline and responsibility, create a budget that details your income, expenses, savings, and investment goals. Then, meticulously adhere to it. Make a financial strategy that considers both your immediate and long-term goals, such as saving for retirement, supporting your education, and building wealth.

FASTLANE FORTUNE

Then, when your priorities and circumstances change, make regular adjustments to your plan.

3. Strategies for Investing

The secret to building and maintaining wealth over time is prudent investment. Create a wise investment plan that takes into account your time horizon, goals, and risk tolerance. Then, diversify your holdings by holding a mix of stocks, bonds, real estate, and alternative investments. When choosing investments, take into account variables including liquidity, volatility, and possible returns. You should also periodically examine and rebalance your portfolio to make sure it stays in line with your objectives and risk tolerance.

4. Tax Guidance

A crucial component of wealth management is tax planning, which lowers your tax obligations and increases the after-tax returns on your investments. Benefit from tax-deferred retirement plans (IRAs and 401(k)s) and investigate tax-efficient investing techniques (such as using tax-advantaged investment vehicles and harvesting capital losses). To find ways to save taxes and create a tax plan that both improves your financial situation and complies with existing tax laws and regulations, speak with a tax counsellor or financial planner.

5. Asset Protection and Risk Management

For the purpose of preserving wealth and guaranteeing long-term financial security, risk mitigation and asset protection are crucial. To guard against unanticipated events and obligations, get enough insurance coverage, such as life, health, and property and casualty insurance. Use asset protection techniques to preserve your assets from creditors, lawsuits, and other risks to your financial security. These techniques include estate planning, asset titling, and trusts.

To lessen your exposure to market volatility and systemic risks, diversify your investments and refrain from placing all of your money into one company.

6. Legacy Preservation and Estate Planning

In order to manage your wealth throughout the generations and protect your legacy for your heirs and beneficiaries in the future, estate planning is essential. Establish a thorough estate plan that includes advance directives, powers of attorney, trusts, and wills to guarantee that your assets are dispersed in accordance with your preferences and to reduce the costs associated with probate and estate taxes. In order to ensure a smooth transfer of wealth and assets, review and update your estate plan on a regular basis to account for changes in your financial objectives, family dynamics, and personal circumstances. You should also let your loved ones know of your intentions and wishes.

7. Generosity and Adopting Needs

Contributing to the community and philanthropic endeavours is a crucial aspect of wealth management, offering advantages in terms of taxes as well as personal fulfilment. Create a plan for your charitable giving that takes into account your beliefs, passions, and financial capabilities. You should also look into philanthropic initiatives that have a significant influence on your neighbourhood and beyond. To optimise tax benefits and streamline your charitable giving efforts, think about setting up a private foundation, charitable trust, or donor-advised fund. These can help you maximise the impact of your contributions.

FASTLANE FORTUNE

*Opening Up Your Fastlane Experience***

It's time to take stock of all the information, ideas, and tactics we've learned to help you achieve financial success and freedom as we near the finish of this life-changing Fastlane adventure. We have examined the tenets and methods of the Fastlane lifestyle throughout this book, from the necessity of wealth creation speed to the significance of striking a balance between short-term rewards and long-term sustainability. We've dug into the minds of prosperous investors, entrepreneurs, and inventors to find the keys to their success and the tactics they use to handle the intricacies of today's business environment.

The Fastlane mentality is centred on a dedication to action, ingenuity, and the unwavering pursuit of one's goals. We now know that success is a process rather than a destination, one that is characterised by tenacity, grit, and an unshakeable faith in one's own capacity for greatness. Regardless of your level of experience as an investor, aspirational professional, or as an entrepreneur, the Fastlane provides a path to long-term financial stability, personal fulfilment, and legacy building.

We started out knowing that wealth creation requires speed and that using velocity, momentum, and invention to achieve quick

FASTLANE FORTUNE

outcomes is crucial. We looked at the shortcomings of standard financial guidance and learned how unorthodox methods and ways of thinking might provide new opportunities and hasten the acquisition of wealth. We gained knowledge on how to spot lucrative prospects, assess the potential of the market, and select the Fastlane route that best fits our objectives, principles, and aspirations.

As we continued along the Fastlane, we learned how to maximise our efforts and attain more effect and scalability by utilising other people's time, money, and skills as well as systems. We studied the wealth acceleration commandments and discovered how to manage time, meet demands, and scale our endeavours for optimal efficacy and efficiency. We learned that developing habits for optimal performance and productivity, accepting risk and unpredictability, and encouraging cooperation and partnerships are crucial for promoting innovation and expansion.

We made a point of stressing the significance of prudent money management, safeguarding assets for the future, and striking a balance between short-term rewards and long-term sustainability during our trip. We discovered how to successfully negotiate the challenges of the Fastlane way of life by accepting setbacks as stepping stones to achievement and cultivating appreciation and awareness along the way. We discussed the value of contributing to society and philanthropic endeavours, realising that genuine riches is found in our beneficial effects on the world around us as much as our tangible belongings.

Remember this when you set out on your own Fastlane journey: success does not always come easily, but it is always worthwhile. Hold fast to your goals, endure hardships head-on, and never lose sight of your infinite potential. You have all you need to unleash your Fastlane adventure and create a life of plenty, prosperity, and fulfilment with the knowledge, skills, and tactics you've received from this book. Take advantage of the chance, rise to the occasion, and start your journey—the Fastlane is waiting for you. Cheers to your prosperity, success, and legacy in life's fast lane.

www.ingramcontent.com/pod-product-compliance
Lightning Source LLC
Chambersburg PA
CBHW050106230526
45470CB00004B/1704